TO·DO·LIST

I0063063

Practical Advice for Starting & Scaling
Your Creative Freelance Business

I NEED THIS!

NEW IDEAS!

CONTRACT

GOOD WORK!

what I enjoy

what I'm good at

values
growth
flexibility
trust

skills!

AMY WEIHER

AW

Book design + composition by Studiolo Secondari

Practical Advice for Starting & Scaling
Your Creative Freelance Business

GOOD
WORK!

AMY
WEIHER

Table of Contents

☑ FIND GOOD CLIENTS

☑ MAKE GOOD MONEY

☑ DO GOOD WORK

☑ NURTURE GOOD GROWTH

DO WHAT YOU *Love*

AND YOU'LL ~~NEVER~~ WORK

A DAY IN YOUR LIFE.

Total bullshit!

Do what you love, as your own boss, and you'll work harder than you ever have before. That doesn't mean you have to be miserable. It's also rewarding as hell and offers perks that will be nearly impossible to find in a traditional nine-to-five. The tips in the pages that follow can help make your self-employment journey a little smoother and easier—and more successful and rewarding. Let's do good work—together!

INTRODUCTION

I never wanted to be a business owner. In grade school I wanted to be a lawyer—they made great money and got to wear fancy suits. In middle school somehow I decided that a racecar driver would be a better job, despite the fact that I don't like going fast or taking risks. In high school, I thought that being an architect might help marry my love of art with my aptitude for math. In college, I studied accounting and art before stumbling across a graphic design class. I finally discovered that there was a way to make a living doing what I loved, but never once did it occur to me that I wouldn't work for someone else.

Yet, twenty years later, here I am. I've got a thriving design studio and support myself along with several people. Pretty amazing. I have flexibility in my schedule. I can take on whatever projects I want. And I don't have to answer to a boss—other than myself.

It hasn't been easy, and I've learned a lot the hard way. The expectations I had when I started this were completely off base in most cases. I envisioned myself working peacefully from a cool-looking office space, with ample time for long lunches, and big projects with bigger budgets that would naturally fall into my lap. But I kept learning and I kept working. As I get older, I'm finally feeling like I've got this mostly figured out—or at least I know better how to navigate the ups and downs—and I wish I could go back in time to tell my younger self a few things that would have made things so much easier. Hence this book.

Whether you're wondering about starting your own freelance business, floundering through the early days, or trying to go from surviving to thriving, my hope is that some of my hard-won lessons can help you avoid some of the pitfalls I hit and build the business of your dreams even faster. While my experience is in graphic design, these ideas and skills are adaptable to a variety of professions, but they are particularly applicable to creative service entrepreneurs. We creatives are a different breed: We're largely driven by our desire to create rather than to simply deliver a product or service. We need to balance our artistic visions with meeting the needs of our clients and the market, which can be difficult on an emotional level as well as a practical one. And many creatives begin their freelancing careers without knowing much about how to actually run a viable business.

How did I get here?

Throughout my childhood and young adult years, I didn't quite know what I wanted to do professionally, but I always knew that I wanted to be a mom. My mom stayed home with my siblings and me and then taught music at our grade school (which horrified me!), so she was always around. My assumption was that I would go to college, get married after graduation, start a job, and then work part-time after we started a family. Best of both worlds, right?

Wrong. Mr. Right was nowhere to be found in college or art school, so I started working at a small advertising firm in New Jersey. The commute was horrible and the pay was lousy, and I lasted three months. My next stop was a small design firm in Philadelphia. The work was great, but there wasn't very much of it, so I was bored a lot. And the money was lousy there too. After a year and a ton of credit card debt, I packed up my stuff and moved back to California.

I settled at a small design firm in Oakland, and that's where I really learned what a business looked like. I got to see the nuts and bolts behind everything from estimating to invoicing to client meetings. I got to really understand what went on behind the scenes from the owner's perspective, and I saw some of the perks of being the boss. My boss came in long after the rest of us had started work and left before we did. She spent her time online shopping and talking to friends when she wasn't art directing, and she generally seemed to be enjoying her day rather than getting through it. I know now what it took for her to be able to get to that point in her career, but at the time I remember being jealous that she had it so easy.

I also learned a lot about what I didn't want at that job. The hours were long—we were expected to *want* to work overtime—and the commute was even longer. The salary was low. There was no flexibility in terms of telecommuting, and we had to use vacation time for things as mundane as a doctor's visit. I hated feeling like every moment of my life was controlled by someone else.

As my three-year employee review neared, I decided that I wanted to work for myself, but I wasn't quite ready to do it full-time. I negotiated a four-day workweek in exchange for ten-hour days and started freelancing a bit on the side. It wasn't much, but it gave me a taste of what could be. One year later, I quit my job and officially launched Weiher Creative.

I was lucky that I had a place to live rent-free for a few months (thanks, Mom and Dad!) and a father who had also made the leap to successful self-employment, so I had a lot of support and a good example to follow. Not everyone has that, and I fully recognize that I am coming from a place of enormous privilege. But success is possible no matter where you're starting from. Whether you have a sudden family inheritance that allows you to quit your job and do what you want, or whether you're broke and unhappy and simply desperate to start something new, you can be your own boss and make it work. My goal is to help you build the wisdom and know-how you need to thrive.

I did eventually get married and have a baby, but my business was ten years old by that point, so neither event really disrupted my work life in a meaningful way. I definitely had to make adjustments to my routines and processes, like getting more help and adjusting my work hours, and I had to figure out how to reprioritize my time, but there was never a question about whether I would keep working for myself. My business is a huge part of who I am, and I never looked back. I love what I do, and I'm grateful that I can make my work and personal lives work together.

The bumpy path to success

I've survived the Great Recession and a global pandemic, and my business has continued to grow throughout all of it. Some of that is because my client list is diverse enough that when one group needs to cut back, other clients need more work. But most of my success is due to hard work and good business practices, which anyone can use to succeed. That's not to say that it has been easy. There have been periods where I wasn't sure where my next client was coming from or if I'd have enough work to stay afloat. I've had clients refuse to pay invoices worth thousands of dollars. I've been so overloaded with work that I've been unsure how I could physically and mentally handle it. I've had unexpected tax bills and computers that suddenly needed to be replaced. But through it all, I've tried to learn lessons from each setback that I can use the next time business gets bumpy—and it will.

I've watched colleagues go out of business or slow to a desperate crawl. I've seen lots of other folks start freelancing with no real idea of what to do or how to do it. Some of those newbies have reached out to me, particularly in the past few years, looking for advice. I tend to hear the same questions over and over in my freelancing groups.

I'm also in the trenches every day, although most days it's not really a slog anymore. Like most small business owners and freelancers, I'm not a millionaire (yet). I don't sit around eating bonbons all day and relaxing while all of my work magically gets done and money just flows into my accounts, but it gets easier and easier to make ends meet. I'm constantly learning new things and growing my skills and the services I can offer, and it's a lot less painful than it used to be.

The lessons ahead

In the pages ahead, I've laid out a list of lessons that I wish I had more fully understood before I started and as my business grew. Knowing these things sooner would have made my working life a lot easier.

If you're not yet a freelancer or are just getting started, the first two sections will help you think about what you want to do, who you want to do it for, and how to set yourself up for success from the beginning. If you've been around a while and are feeling good about what you're doing, you may want to skip most of that. I recommend periodically taking the time to reevaluate, especially if you're feeling stagnant. My business and what I want out of it have changed over time, and reviewing these questions is helpful when I'm feeling stuck or unsure of where I want to go.

Following the first section are practical tips and guidance related to managing money, finding and working with clients, the day-to-day challenges of doing good work, and continually building your business. I'll share helpful information my colleagues and I have learned the hard way, both practical and personal, that you can apply to your own situations. My hope is that this book will serve as an ongoing resource for you so that as issues come along, you can flip through to the tip you need now.

Let's get started!

FIND OUT WHAT YOU LIKE DOING BEST

BEST

AND FIND SOMEONE TO PAY $ YOU FOR DOING IT. Almost...

— KATHARINE WHITEHORN

... but not quite. The better choice is to find out what you like doing best, ask what people need, and figure out where those two things overlap. That's your sweet spot and the focus of the next section.

BUILD A GOOD FOUNDATION

Start with a reality check.

Starting a business is easy. *Running* a business is hard work, and it's a job. If you're reading this book, you likely already have the self-employment itch or are wondering about setting out on your own. But that doesn't necessarily mean that you're cut out for it or that it's even what you really want. If someone is pushing toward your own business by forcing you to read this book, beware of external motivation! You have to want it because you'll be the one doing the work.

Before you quit your job, think about the work you do and the business you daydream about. Take your time mulling over these questions.

- Why do you want to start a business? What desires would it fill for you that your current job isn't, like more free time, a flexible work schedule, more control over your work, or working on a passion project? Can you get any of those by talking to your current boss or finding a new position elsewhere?

- Assuming you're starting something that's related to your current occupation, what are the parts of your job that you like best? What are the parts that you like least?
- If you could design the perfect job for yourself, what would it look like? What would it absolutely not include?
- Do you have any experience with running a business or doing any behind-the-scenes business tasks? How did it go? What did you learn?
- Is your business idea viable? Do people want or need what you offer? Is the need already being adequately met by others? How will you differentiate your service or offering to stand out? What research do you need to do to understand the market?
- Do you have any experience working in the type of business you're thinking about? If not, what training or education will you need in advance and as you go?
- Do you have access to other people who have done this before who can help or advise you? What advice do they have to offer?
- Do you have any customers now? Where will you find more? Who are your target clients? How will you let them know what you have to offer?
- Are you disciplined enough to get up every day and do what needs to be done, or do you need a lot of external motivation?
- Are you driven and resourceful enough to keep going when things suck—because they will? Think of times you've faced a big obstacle. What did you do well? Where did you struggle?
- Can you handle the uncertainty of an irregular paycheck? Do you have cash reserves? How do you handle uncertainty mentally and emotionally?
- How do you handle failure? What skills and support do you need to develop to become more resilient?
- How do you handle distractions? What are your usual distractions? How might you avoid them?
- How do you feel about risk? Do you tend to plan and worry, or do you jump in without doing much thinking and preparing?
- Do you have a support network—spouse, family, mentor, best friend, etc.—to help you financially, mentally, and emotionally? Do you know others in your field who can share ideas and encourage you professionally?
- Are you willing to put in the time and effort it takes to market yourself and get more work? How will you start? Would you rather be a worker bee who does work that someone else acquires?
- What is the best thing that could happen if you strike out on your own? How could you set yourself up for this best-case scenario?

- What is the worst thing that could happen? What ways can you plan for that in advance and have solutions ready?
- What are your strengths and weaknesses? Do you know how to manage them well? Does your personality lend itself to the entrepreneurial lifestyle? See the Personality Traits sidebar on the following page.

Be brutally honest with yourself about these questions, even as you plan and dream. If the answers to some of these aren't compatible with running your own show, is there an existing job that might give you some of what you want without having to do it yourself? Or are there guardrails you can put in place to help you? Knowing your limitations is the key to crafting your plan for success. While you can't anticipate many problems, looking ahead as best you can prevents some problems and builds your problem-solving mindset.

Five Benefits of Being Your Own Boss

1. **Time.** Your time is your own, and you can set your own schedule. There may be some limitations depending on your industry, but in general you decide when you'll work and when you won't. Want to sleep in, take a long lunch, play hooky, or take an extended absence? You can decide to do that too.
2. **Choice.** You can decide what clients to work with and what projects to work on. You can decide if you want to work in broader industries or really specific niche markets. You can decide if you grow a team or stay solo. You aren't trapped by existing workflows or procedures. Everything is up to you.
3. **Money.** When you're the boss, you can charge what you want, and you're only constrained by the number of hours in the day or the amount of work you can produce (and of course, what the market will bear). Without the limitations of a set paycheck or hourly wage, you can decide what you'd like to earn and make your own financial goals a reality.
4. **Location.** It's up to you whether you want to work from your kitchen, a coffee shop, or the patio of a rented villa in Italy. Don't feel like commuting? You don't have to. With a laptop and a Wi-Fi connection, you can work from pretty much anywhere. (Again, some industries have limits here.)
5. **Flexibility.** Life happens, and as we saw throughout the pandemic, things can change at a moment's notice. It's easier to adjust and respond when you're in charge. Need to pick up a sick kid from school or switch

vendors because of a supply chain issue? You can do that—without asking your boss's permission!

Five Downsides of Being Your Own Boss

1. **Accountability.** When things go wrong—and they will—it's on you to fix it. Even if it's not your fault. The buck stops with you, and everything and everyone that relates to your business reflects you. Your reputation is on the line in every interaction you have with the outside world (even if it doesn't seem business-related), which can feel a bit overwhelming at times.

2. **Hat-wearing.** When you're on your own, you wear all the hats and are responsible for all of the jobs, even if you're paying someone else to do them. Accounting, marketing, human resources, business development, estimating, billing, project management, and customer service are just some of the tasks that need to be done in every business—and that's on top of the actual work you do.

3. **Money.** Many business owners experience cycles of feast and famine. Sometimes they don't know where their next check is coming from (especially in the beginning). Cash flow and budgeting are really important without a steady paycheck. Taking time off takes more planning and preparation when you don't have paid vacation time.

4. **Uncertainty.** The flip side of flexibility is uncertainty. When things change unexpectedly, you need to be ready to pick up the pieces or move in a different direction. Clients cancel contracts at the last minute. You might get sick or have an accident and be unable to work for a few weeks. Computers fry and files disappear. There are no guarantees, and business owners need to be prepared for the worst at any given time, both practically and emotionally.

5. **Burnout.** When you're working for someone else, you can often leave the office at the end of the day and leave work behind. But when you're working for yourself, it's harder to do. There is *always* something that needs to be done, decided, or delegated. Depending on your workload and life situation, it can be hard to shut down and stop working—and even harder to stop thinking about work even when you're technically out of the office. It can feel like you're always on, even with really good boundaries in place. This takes a day-to-day toll, and if you don't take steps to manage the stress it can escalate into full-blown burnout.

Personality traits that make for successful entrepreneurs

How many of these sound like you? Where do you need to stretch and grow?

✓ **Highly self-motivated.** Are you a go-getter who can do what needs to be done without prodding from another person? Can you figure out what needs to be done and do it without being told how? And can you do that day after day?

✓ **Like being in control.** Do you want to make all of the decisions and shoulder the responsibility? Do you hate being told what to do?

✓ **Open to taking risks.** Starting a business is inherently risky, and running a business requires taking risks on a regular basis—some bigger than others. Are you open to taking the leap when needed?

✓ **Good with money.** Are you good at setting and following a budget? Can you manage cash flow? Does money burn a hole in your pocket, or do you prefer to save for a rainy day?

✓ **Ethical and honest.** Do you do the right thing even when no one is watching? Are you honest even when it's inconvenient or difficult? Do you have a strong value system that guides you and the work that you do?

✓ **Flexible.** Are you able to compromise and collaborate? Can you pivot and make changes on the fly when the unexpected happens?

✓ **Driven.** Do you strive to reach bigger and better goals? Do you dream about reaching the next level? Are you competitive and determined to do things better and outlast your competition?

✓ **Disciplined.** Do you hang in there when the going gets tough or you don't feel like doing the work? Are you willing to follow through even when you'd rather be doing other things?

✓ **Creative.** Are you a problem solver? Do you have the imagination to think inside and outside the box to address challenges? Are you energized by finding new and better ways to do things?

✓ **Confident.** Are you confident both in yourself and in your service or product? Can you persuade others to buy what you're selling (both literally and figuratively)? How do you feel about yourself when you make mistakes or things go wrong?

✓ **Willing to fail.** When things go wrong, both large and small, how do you respond? Can you accept criticism and learn from your mistakes? Are you able to distinguish between failures that are your own versus those due to forces beyond your control?

✓ **Curious.** Do you know what you don't know and where to learn more? Are you open to learning new ideas and different ways of doing things? Do you get excited by keeping up with the latest innovations in your industry?

✓ **Resilient.** How do you handle adversity? Do you keep calm and carry on or freak out and shut down? How well do you handle conflict? How do you feel when you have to go back to the drawing board?

✓ **Visionary.** Are you dreaming of a quick windfall or playing the long game? Do you have a vision of where you want to take your business and the patience and time to get there? Can you identify the major milestones along the way?

TAKE THE *Next Step*

GOOD

☐ Spend some time thinking about the questions above. Note any particular feelings or thoughts that come up.

BETTER

☐ Print out the worksheets for section one (goodworkbook.com) and thoroughly answer them. Make a note of any aha! items or items that give you pause.

BEST

☐ Come up with your own list of additional pros and cons for your situation. Can you think of solutions to help you overcome the cons?

Consider the kind of work you want to do.

I'm presuming you're coming into this with a pretty clear sense of what you do overall. You already know you're a writer, designer, or illustrator. Drilling down from there, what kinds of projects do you want to work on? Spend some time thinking about past work you've enjoyed.

- What type of project was it?
- What industry was it in?
- What kind of client was it—a big corporate client, a small nonprofit, or a small business?
- Was there a personality trait, type of person, or style of working that appealed to you?
- Were there lots of moving parts or a single type of deliverable?
- Who else was involved in the project? What roles did they play? What were they like to work with?
- How much did it pay? Or did you feel like you were rewarded well for your time?
- What sort of timeline did it have?
- How much creative freedom did you have?
- What was the end result like?
- Why is it one of your favorites?

Once you've answered those questions for a few projects, look for patterns. If your favorite projects tend to be designing social media ads for pet sitters or writing annual reports for hospitals, notice that. It'll help you hone your skills and know how to better market yourself. You don't have to do that type of work exclusively, but life is short and business can be hard. If there's a type of project that gets you more excited than the rest, then do more of that.

For years, I really resisted being upfront about choosing a niche market. I heard over and over how important it was to narrow down my focus to a particular industry to be seen as the expert in that area. But all I could see was the business lost. If I choose one market, won't I alienate everyone else? What if a different type of client has a great project that I want to work on? What if nobody in my target market wants to work with me and I starve to death at my desk?!? Over the years I've learned just because you focus on one type of work doesn't mean you can't work with anyone else. You can choose to say yes to anyone or anything at any time, and most clients are attracted to your overall skills not your particular target market.

I love working with nonprofits, particularly schools. The very first line on my website (in big, bold, blue type) says: "We help nonprofits do good—better." So when a prospect at a nonprofit organization is looking for a graphic designer who works with people just like them, it's clear from the start that I'm their gal. But that doesn't mean that I don't work with anyone else. In fact, some of my favorite and busiest clients are for-profit companies (who are awesome people to work with). Even though I'm intentional about who my target is, the language I use in my marketing is inclusive enough for other people to see themselves in it too. "Design for Good Causes and Good People with Good Intentions." Who can't see themselves in that?

Just like everything else, your target market may change over time. You may find yourself working with clients ten years from now that you can't even fathom serving today. Perhaps your interests will change, or perhaps your chosen industry will evolve. Alternatively, as in the following example, you might discover an entirely new, underserved market and step in to fill the gap.

Avivit Fisher, owner of REdD Strategy Marketing Consultancy, started out doing marketing for small businesses in general. After a personal tragic event, she decided to focus on working specifically with mental health professionals. "In 2015 my house burned down in a fire, and I was trying to find someone that would help me deal with what I was going through emotionally. It was very difficult to find a therapist through my online research, and I saw the gap between what people are searching for online and how therapists present themselves. I wanted to help therapists close this gap through marketing and decided to focus specifically on private practice owners."

The flip side of finding who you want to work with is to also get clear on what work you *don't* want to do. That might even be more important since you'll be miserable working on stuff you don't like, and it'll drain your energy for other work. When I first started, I prided myself on being a one-stop shop. Clients could come to me with any project and I'd get it done, even if it wasn't totally in my wheelhouse. I ended up doing a bit of everything. I realized pretty quickly that I absolutely hated doing animation and website coding. So I stopped doing those myself. It's more efficient and less draining to get an expert to do it, and clients benefit from work done well, no matter who does it. It can feel hard to turn down work, especially when you're starting out or in a slow spell, but I've found that the frustration and drained energy are almost never worth the money. My time and energy would be better spent looking for better work.

Once you're clear on what you don't want to do, decide if you're willing to partner with someone else you trust who will do that work. I have continued to offer website design and development over the years because I have great relationships with coders I trust. I still don't love doing them because I don't understand the nitty-gritty of how the development works and can't fix it if something goes wrong with the developer. I still consider removing that service from my offerings, but my mixed feelings are OK. I don't have to chase web projects, and when I'm contacted about doing one, I can decide on a case-by-case basis if it's something I want to do. Knowing how I feel about it makes my decisions easier.

These days I consider myself a one-stop shop in a different way. If it's not something I can (or want to) do, I can either bring on someone to do the work for me or I can refer the project to someone else. Either way, I'm someone who can help solve a problem—that's what clients want most.

Again, keep this in mind: all of this can change. What you like to do today might not be what you want to do tomorrow. Be open to surprises. Life changes; businesses change; people learn new things. Maybe a pandemic will come along and shut down the industry you work for or open an opportunity you never considered. You have the power to change your mind and change your business. No day job will give you that.

Not sure if you want to take on a particular project or type of work? Consider these questions.

1. What does the deadline or turnaround time look like? Do I have the time to work on this project? What does my schedule look like if I say yes or no? Is there flexibility to customize the timeframe to my needs?
2. How do I feel about the client? Is it someone I like working with or am I feeling red flags in my gut? Do I feel connected to them personally?
3. Is the work interesting to me or in an area I feel passionate about? Is it a type of project that I'd like to do more of?
4. Is there enough budget? If not, is there another reason to say yes (good experience, portfolio piece, passion project, foot in the door, etc.)?
5. Do I have the expertise to take this on? Is it something I know how to do and feel comfortable doing, or is there a learning curve involved? Where will I get help if I need it?
6. Will I need to bring in other people to work on this with me? Have I worked with them before? How much extra time and effort will that project management add on my part?
7. Do I have the mental bandwidth to take this on? Am I already stressed out due to other projects or clients, or is this no big deal?
8. What does my gut say? Trust it. Over time you'll learn what's most important to you and what red flags you absolutely can't ignore.

TAKE THE *Next Step*

☑ ☑

GOOD

☐ Think about your favorite type of project and write down some notes about what makes it ideal (download the worksheet at goodworkbook.com). Do you want to do that only type of work or focus on it among other projects?

BETTER

☐ Update your elevator pitch to focus on the work you most want to do. (See the "Brainstorm Your Brand" chapter.)

BEST

☐ Update your website and marketing materials with your new focus so that your desired prospects know what kinds of work they should hire you to do.

NOTES

Think about who you want to work with.

Now that you have some clarity on what you want to do, who do you want to do it for? When you're choosing your work, you're choosing your coworkers and partners and project bosses—and people make a huge difference in how a project goes.

Spend some time thinking about past clients you've enjoyed working with.

- Who were they?
- What were their personalities like?
- How did they communicate? How did they handle any conflicts, questions, or clarifications?
- How did they treat you, both as a person and as a vendor or partner?
- Did they appreciate the work you did? How did they show it?
- Did they value what you had to offer and listen to what you had to say? How did they show they trusted you?
- Were they respectful of your time? How did you communicate with them about timing and the schedule?
- Did they respect the budget and pay on time? How did they negotiate, if needed?
- Did you have things in common with them, both related to the work and beyond it?
- Where did they work—what region or industry?
- What were their job titles? Where did they fall in the structure of their organization?
- How much did they know about your industry or your type of work? Did they listen to what you needed to explain about the process and result?
- What help did they need from you?
- What were they passionate about?
- Why did you like working with them?
- Did you enjoy the work itself? Do you want to do more of that kind of work? Were you happy with the result?

Again, look for patterns. Maybe your ideal clients are women in their forties with big personalities who are married with kids and are vice presidents in corporations. Or maybe they're mechanical engineers in Midwest startups who are introverted and shy. Knowing who you want to work with will also help you figure out where to direct your marketing efforts and what to say to connect with them—we'll focus on that in the next section.

Having a target kind of client doesn't mean you won't work with anyone else or that it'll always be roses when your ideal client calls. But it makes things so much easier when you have an idea of who is right for you and then surround yourself with those people.

TAKE THE Next Step

GOOD

☐ Think about someone you really enjoyed working with/for and write down some notes about what made them so awesome (download the worksheet at goodworkbook.com).

BETTER

☐ Update your elevator pitch to include the types of clients you want to work with. (See the "Brainstorm Your Brand" chapter.)

BEST

☐ Update your website and marketing materials with your new focus so that your desired prospects see themselves as potential clients.

Choose your location.

During the pandemic, millions of people suddenly started working from home and discovered working from home is vastly different than being in an office. A laptop perched on the corner of the kitchen table might be OK for a while but likely isn't sustainable. Lucky for you, you're planning to be your own boss and can set yourself up wherever you like.

Depending on the type of business you're starting, one of the first questions to figure out is where you'll work. The great thing about owning a creative service business is that you can pretty much do it anywhere. Figure out what you need to do your best work. Some of this depends on the type of business you're starting. Some of it has to do with your personality and life situation. Consider these questions about the details of your business.

- Will you have employees?
- Will you have in-person client meetings?
- Is image important? Is being located in a specific city or neighborhood important to your clientele?
- How much privacy do you need? Are you a lawyer or a therapist that needs to keep conversations confidential?

Based on the answers above, you may need to think about getting equipment like sound-muffling wall panels, a sound machine for the hallway, a document scanner, selfie lighting and a good microphone, a couch or other comfortable group seating ... the list goes on!

For me, I need a home office with plenty of space for file cabinets, bookshelves, printing equipment, and a large standing desk/treadmill combo. I have two twenty-four–inch monitors on my desk and really good Wi-Fi. Most importantly for me? My office has a door. It doesn't necessarily keep my son out while I'm in meetings, but it does give me some separation and privacy, especially with a husband who works from home too. That door also is a barrier between work life and home life—we'll talk more about these vital boundaries later. With some exceptions, when I'm not working I can shut the door and leave the office behind (as much as any self-employed person can do), and it's important to my work and my personal life that I do this the best I can.

Your list will look different, and you might not be able to have everything you'd like up front—I didn't either. But know your basic requirements for a good workstation (chair, desk, internet, computer) and start there.

I agonized for an unnecessarily long time over where I should locate my business. I knew I'd be working from a bedroom at my parents' house to start with, but hopefully wouldn't be there for more than a few months. Should I list their street address and then change it later, or get a PO box or a mailbox at a UPS store and drive to get my mail every day? What if I moved somewhere further away? Is it safe to put my street address out there? Will clients try to show up at random? Does a house address look less professional than an office address?

I didn't need to worry about any of that. I went with my parents' address to start, nobody ever showed up there, and it was a breeze to update throughout all of the other moves I've made since. People move and addresses are easy to change. Thanks to the pandemic and more people working from home, any questions about whether you're a professional if you're on a laptop in your living room are pretty much removed. If you have an actual office or storefront, then the decision is easy. If you don't want your address made public, that's fine too—lots of companies don't advertise anything other than a website, email, and phone number. So just pick something to start. You can always change it later.

If you're not working at home, make sure to consider all the costs when choosing a location. Can you and any employees or contractors work remotely, or do people really need to come into the office? Do your customers really care where you're located, or do you just think they do? How much (if any) does the way your office looks matter?

When Jean started her interior design firm her biggest mistake was not thinking more critically about some of these questions. "I work with wealthy homeowners and thought I needed to impress my clients, so I rented a fancy space in one of the priciest areas in Northern California and hired local employees to be in the office. Despite working eighteen-hour days to try to make ends meet, I struggled to make it work financially. When the pandemic hit, it saved me in a way—I gave up the expensive office, and as employees have moved on, I've replaced them with remote talent at more affordable rates."

Do keep in mind though that you need to conform to local zoning laws, even if you're working out of your house. So do a quick check with your city's department of city planning just to make sure you're in the clear. For example, in Snohomish County, Washington, a home business doesn't need a county license unless it engages in a regulated activity (like a pawn broker) and is in an unincorporated area (outside of a city—they have a map). In my particular city, certain types of home-based businesses aren't allowed (like retail stores) and others are (tutors who instruct no more than one student at a time).

You may not be able to control every aspect of your location, but leverage your flexibility and count the costs of your decisions to make the most of your situation.

TAKE THE
☑ *Next Step* ☑

GOOD

☐ Write down your minimum requirements for a workspace—consider your equipment needs and also ambient factors like comfort and noise level. Then think about your dream workspace. Where is it? What do you need to create it?

BETTER

☐ Consider your options and try working in a few different locations (they might be different rooms in your house, coffeehouses, or other workspaces).

☐ Purchase any critical equipment or software that you don't already have.

BEST

☐ Create the ideal space where you can do your best work. Build it up (slowly, if you have to) so that you can expand and treat yourself as you grow.

NOTES

Create your schedule.

Many freelancers start out as employees and then get the itch to go out on their own. For most of us, being an employee meant being required to be in an office, sitting at a desk from 9 a.m. to 5 p.m. or 8 a.m. to 6 p.m. or some version of that. Those standard working hours can be a really hard habit to break when you're on your own. When I first started out, I felt like I had to be immediately available to anyone who emailed or called during the day, and I felt like my clients would know if I was taking a break and think I was a slacker. Even twenty years later, I still tend to stay at my desk all day, even when work is slow. I sometimes have to remind myself that I can go do something else if I want.

When you're the boss, you can work hours that make sense for you. Do you start at 11 a.m. and work until dinner? Do you work in the morning and again at night when the kids are in bed? Think about what your ideal day looks and feels like. Consider when you're most productive and creative. If you tend to feel energized and motivated at a certain time of day, capitalize on it.

Your workday could be dictated in part by where you live, what industries you serve, and where your clients live, but as long as you're available at some point during the day when they are, you make the rules.

Consider whether you'll be available on weekends, and what that looks like. One of my regular contractors only works on weekends, so I load her up with projects on Friday night and it's ready for me on Sunday. A landscape designer I know works from Tuesday through Saturday because Saturday is when she meets clients at the nursery to pick out plants. I usually do at least a little bit of work on weekends, whether for myself or my clients, but with a catch—I never tell my clients I'm doing it, and I never send emails or return phone calls during that time. The last thing I want is for clients to expect me to work on the weekend, but if it works for you, go for it!

Think about meetings too. Clients and prospects will want to schedule time with you. When works best for you? Just because you're at work during your scheduled open time, it doesn't necessarily mean you're available and ready to jump on a call. Creatives in particular need solid, focused time to get in the flow and get work done. Honor that.

What does that look like for me? On a typical day, I'm at my desk from about 7:30 a.m. until 5:30 p.m., but I drop off my son at school around 9 a.m. and then pick him up at 3:30 p.m. I usually have some PTA stuff to attend to when I'm at the school, so I schedule meetings with clients between 10 a.m. and 2:30 p.m., which gives me some buffer on either end. I don't like meetings early in the morning when I'm still waking up or at the end of the workday when I'm more mentally tired, so I don't offer that as an option unless an exception needs to be made. A few years ago, I started blocking off Mondays and Fridays, too, just because I felt like it. Who wants to meet on a Friday afternoon? Not me!

Make sure you're clear about when you're available, especially if it's not the typical workday that folks are used to, so that people know what to expect. And if you're at all tempted to apologize for any schedule limitations you have, don't. Your schedule is yours, and what you do with the rest of your time is nobody's business. Be clear, not apologetic, about when you're available.

TAKE THE Next Step

GOOD

☐ Look at your existing obligations and the clients on your roster (or the ones that you want to have on your list). How do they impact or influence a potential work schedule?

BETTER

☐ Decide when you will make yourself available for meetings. Consider the time you have open, time zone differences with clients, and your energy levels and personal preferences.

BEST

☐ Update your website with your general work schedule and meeting availability so that people know what to expect. An online calendar is a great way to let people know exactly when they can schedule a meeting with you, no explanations needed.

Set yourself up for success.

OK, you're gonna start a business. Woo-hoo! It's easy to get started—really!—but there are a few business essentials that you'll want to work out and get set up properly before you dive in. You'll thank yourself later on.

I am not a lawyer or a tax professional, so I'm keeping it simple and general. There are lots of available resources and places to get help, and I've listed some of those here too. If there are elements of your business you're unsure about, ask questions now to prevent headaches later.

Do you need a business plan?

Maybe, maybe not. I didn't, other than a vague idea that I wanted to work on my own while my future kids slept, and I wasn't interested in having employees. I wasn't looking for funding or partners, so a business plan wasn't a requirement. I think it's a good idea to have some sort of idea of where you eventually want to take your business (maybe a list of goal, if you like), but it's not a requirement unless someone is asking you for it.

Even if it's not required, doing a business plan might be helpful for certain personality types—those who love planning and working through the details in advance or, conversely, those who are too apt to wing it and end up missing important details. A business plan can help you set up milestones and think objectively as you make decisions too.

If you do decide to write an official plan, there are lots of resources and examples online that can help you. These are just a few:

- The US Small Business Administration (SBA) has lots of resources, including courses on how to write a plan, plan templates you can customize, and other planning guides: www.sba.gov
- If you need more hands-on help, the SBA has a list of resource partners that can provide training, mentors, and counseling: https://www.sba.gov/local-assistance/resource-partners. Some of these resources are specifically geared towards women and veterans.
- The SBA website can help you find your local Small Business Development Center (SBDC) for individualized counseling and local resources: https://www.sba.gov/local-assistance/resource-partners/small-business-development-centers-sbdc.
- USA.gov also has resources for small businesses (www.usa.gov/small-business). From there, I can get information about how to

start, grow, or fund a business in a specific state, and I can view contracting opportunities.

- There are also lots of companies online you can pay to write a plan for you if the free resources above aren't quite what you need. A quick search will give you options.
- Consider looking at other entrepreneurs' plans too. Even if they provide a different service than you do, their plans might give ideas to help shape your own.

Do you need funding?

Generally, yes, but how much depends on the kind of business you're starting. Running a solo content writing business out of your guest bedroom is a lot less expensive than starting a freelance design firm in a rented office. Have an honest money conversation with yourself, your family, and any business partners or other stakeholders before you dive in and plan ahead. Yes, starting a business is a risk, but there's a limit to how risky you need to be. Ask these questions.

- How will you support yourself as you get going? Do you have a savings cushion to cover you for a specific amount of time, or will someone lend you money or cover your expenses for a while?
- Will you start your business part-time and build slowly while you have a separate income, or will you dive in and rely solely on the business from the start?
- What expenses will you have, both for the business and yourself? Will a spouse or partner cover the personal portion, or do you need to be able to cover everything?
- What equipment or supplies do you need? How often do you need to purchase those? How often might they need servicing or repairs? Are there associated costs (like printer ink or special printer paper) that might be regularly needed too?
- What business startup costs are there—licensing fees, website costs, legal fees, etc.?
- Will you need to buy or subscribe to any software?
- Will you need storage space for any inventory?
- Will you need to purchase or lease a vehicle? Does it need special insurance?
- Will you rely on other vendors or services to provide materials or products? Are those one-time costs or ongoing expenses?
- Will you have employees or contractors? How much will that cost?

- Do you need benefits, for yourself or other people? How will you get them and at what cost?
- If you're finding an office or rental space for your business, does the location affect the costs? Are tax rates a little lower in the next town? What about property taxes or rental rates? Are there creative ways you can use space or partner with another business to cut costs? Can you rent a desk in a coworking space?
- Do you need to get a bank loan or line of credit to cover costs? Will you have investors? What sort of paperwork or collateral will funding sources require? Who can you turn to for advice on things like this?
  - → Check out the SBA. Their website has an entire section dedicated to different kinds of funding programs: https://www.sba.gov/funding-programs.
  - → Reach out to your local Small Business Development Center (SBDC) for advice and funding resources: https://www.sba.gov/local-assistance/resource-partners/small-business-development-centers-sbdc.
  - → Talk to your accountant or financial planner to get a full picture of your current finances and recommendations on what you can spend without jeopardizing your future.
  - → Talk to your bank about loan options.
  - → Find small business forums on Facebook and LinkedIn and find out what other business owners are doing.

It's important to be honest with yourself, even having a plan to end your business. How long will you or can you give yourself to make the business work? If you're not making a profit in a certain amount of time, will you call it quits or get new funding?

These can be hard, even disheartening, conversations, but what they're really doing is preparing you for success. If you know the bare-bones reality, you can make a plan to face it and avoid worst-case scenarios.

How will your business be structured?

How you structure your business will impact your registration requirements, tax rates, and personal liability. Different business structures affect how much you'll pay in taxes, how you can or can't raise money, what paperwork you need to file, and how much of your personal property might be at risk if something goes wrong. Consider what is the best balance for you before you register your business with the state.

Start by visiting the SBA website for information on each of the business structures listed below. Visit to your local SBDC to talk with an advisor. A business advisor, attorney or accountant can give you the pros and cons of each type of business structure for your specific situation, and they can let you know how easy or difficult it'll be to change later on.

- **Sole proprietorship**. These are easy to form—you're automatically considered a sole proprietor as soon as you start doing business activities. The good thing about being a sole proprietor is that you're the boss—you have complete control over your business. The bad thing? You're not considered a separate business entity, so you can be held personally responsible for any and all business debts and obligations—that includes your personal assets too. So if something goes really wrong, you could lose your personal assets (like a house or your savings) as a result. For a lot of consultants just starting out, that's not a huge risk, and a sole proprietorship is a great way to test the waters and see if your business is viable before moving to a more formal structure.
- **Partnerships.** These can be either limited (LP) or limited liability (LLP) and are good choices for businesses with multiple owners and groups of professionals (like attorneys). In general, these partnerships limit the control that members have over the company and also limit the liability that each member is responsible for—for example, they're not responsible for the actions of the other partners.
- **Limited Liability Company (LLC).** An LLC lets you get some of the benefits of being a corporation (protection from personal liability with separate personal and business assets) without the corporate taxes. LLCs are a good choice if you have significant personal assets to protect and if you want to pay lower taxes than you would in a corporation.
- **Corporations (S, C, B).** This structure offers the strongest protection against personal liability. Corporations are considered legal entities that are totally separate from their owners. They're expensive to start, and require more extensive paperwork and reporting. Still, they have some tax advantages. The different types of corporations all have different startup requirements, so a tax professional can outline the differences and help you figure out whether incorporating makes sense for you.

I was a sole proprietor for thirteen years before incorporating. One thing I was surprised about when I started? Self-employment taxes. The self-employment tax funds Social Security and Medicare, and they're often called the FICA taxes (Federal Insurance Contributions Act). As of this writing, the self-employment tax rate is 15.3 percent of your net earnings. Everyone who works has to pay FICA taxes, but the difference between being working for yourself and working for someone else is that employers are required to pay half of that tax. When you're self-employed, the government views you as both employer and employee, so you pay the full tax yourself. What that boils down to is that being your own boss will cost you about 7.65 percent in additional taxes—that's on top of the usual federal, state, and local income taxes you pay. You can cut down that tax burden a bit through deductions, but the best way to do it is to incorporate. An accountant can help you figure out the best plan of action for you.

Gabrielle Ianniello learned about business structure and liability the hard way when starting her Corporate Quitter podcast. "For one, I didn't know *anything* about business finances, legal structures, etc. I spent the first year of my business not really operating as a business, using up all my personal savings and racking up $40K of personal debt just to build my platform and float through the exploration phase. Had I known the benefit of leveraging business debt/credit and establishing an LLC or corporation early on, I probably would've avoided a lot of the financial headaches I'm experiencing now. I'm finally in a place where I've stopped the bleeding financially, but it's going to take a bit of time to pay off debt, build savings/cash reserves, and repair my credit."

No accountant? No attorney? No advisor? No problem!

There are lots of ways to find someone good to help you.

- ✓ Ask friends, family, and coworkers who they use. Additionally, talk to other local small business owners, especially if they're in a similar line of work to yours. Get a list of three or four recommendations and interview them.
- ✓ Search the IRS business directory (https://www.irs.gov/businesses).
- ✓ Check your local and state tax and business associations.
- ✓ Do a search for local vendors and see what sorts of comments/ratings they have on Yelp (with a grain of salt, of course).
- ✓ Look at the chamber of commerce and local colleges and universities. Who is speaking at business lunches or teaching classes at the business school? They're likely reputable and worth checking out.

Get registered

Your location, business type, and industry will dictate what you need to register. If you're conducting your business as a sole proprietorship using your legal name, then you and your business are considered one and the same and you won't need to register anywhere. If your sole proprietorship uses a name other than your own, your state may require you to register the name of your company (known as *doing business as* or DBA). For most small businesses, getting registered is as simple as registering your business name with state and local governments. You will need to file to get a federal tax number (see the next section), and if you want to trademark your name you'll want to file with the United States Patent and Trademark Office. Nonprofit organizations need to register as a tax-exempt entity with the IRS. Find out what is required for your situation by visiting your city and state government websites or the Secretary of State website for your state.

Get an employer identification number (EIN)

An EIN is the unique federal tax number used to identify your business. It can also help you register as a business entity, obtain business loans, open bank accounts, and more. It's not necessarily required unless you're going to hire employees, take over an existing business, or form a partnership, LLC, or corporation. But it's a good idea to get one, and it's free.

Not sure if you need one? The IRS has a handy "Do You Need an EIN?" questionnaire that you can fill out to get the answer: https://www.irs.gov/businesses/small-businesses-self-employed/do-you-need-an-ein.

Even if you aren't required to get one, there are lots of benefits to getting an EIN:

1. An EIN helps prevent identity theft. An EIN separates your personal finances from your business finances—once you have an EIN, you don't need to provide vendors or clients with your social security number (SSN) and can keep that information private. I used my SSN on my taxes for years (I'd never even heard of an EIN). One morning a client left one of my signed W-9 forms in a folder on the front seat of her unlocked car in downtown Oakland, and it got stolen (duh!). It was a pain in the behind to report it to the police and the IRS, and even though I now use an EIN, my social security number is out in the wild, occasionally causing trouble and requiring me to reset passwords and cancel credit cards. Every year at tax time, I have to get special pin numbers from the IRS to make sure that no one else is filing fake taxes in my name. Keep in mind

that EIN numbers are already public information and can still be stolen and used fraudulently, but it's not nearly as common as SSN theft.

2. An EIN gives you more credibility and makes you look more established and serious about your business. It also helps prove that you're an independent contractor rather than an employee, which can make you more attractive to clients who may need to prove to the IRS that they've classified you properly when they're paying taxes.

3. An EIN can help you at tax time. Want to deduct that home office space on your taxes? An EIN shows the IRS that you're a legitimate business, which could lower your chances of getting audited.

4. Some banks require an EIN for business accounts. When I started out, getting separate business and personal bank accounts was easy. That's not necessarily the case today. Some banks require an EIN to open business checking and savings accounts. If you'll want to open a business line of credit, you'll definitely need one.

5. To hire employees, you need an EIN. Even if you're not sure whether you'll eventually hire employees, getting an EIN now allows you to easily scale your business and set up payroll when you're ready.

What licenses and permits do you need?

Most jurisdictions require that any businesses operating within their bounds have a business license, regardless of the type of business. The types of licenses required vary depending on your industry and location, so you'll need to do a little research to find out what your state, county, and city require. For example, if I visit the Washington State Department of Revenue website, and click on "Get Licensing Requirements," I can answer a series of questions that will result in a really handy list of what licenses I'll need and links to where to get each one.

If your state charges sales tax, you may also need a seller's permit (certificate of resale). Services aren't taxed, but if you're selling an actual thing or marking up printed items before you deliver them to the customer, then you'll need to charge sales tax and have a permit. Consult your accountant or the state tax authorities at your state's department of revenue if you're not sure what you need, and then you can apply through forms that are usually online. Get help and make sure you're compliant from the start so you can avoid costly issues down the road.

Do you need business insurance?

That'll depend on the kind of business you're running, personal preference for risk, and any legal requirements from the state or federal government or from your clients. Start by asking yourself two questions:

1. Do you have a lot of inventory and other business property that would be difficult to replace on your own? If all you have is a single laptop, then you likely don't need insurance. If you have thousands of dollars of expensive computer equipment, you likely can't afford to replace that on your own.
2. Is there a reasonable chance your business could be sued for a large amount of money? Could someone get injured or have an accident on your property, or might you have a data breach, or could something you design or make have errors or be defective?

If you can say yes to either of those questions, insurance can minimize the risks. I have general business liability insurance for myself. I originally got it because I occasionally had meetings with clients in my home and wanted to help protect our assets if there was ever an accident (like if a client tripped on my porch and sued me). I also have additional certificates of insurance for various clients that require them—they tell me how much insurance I need to work with them, and I add them to my policy. If you're not sure what you need, talk to your insurance agent, business advisor, or accountant. You can also talk to other business owners in your field.

Open a business bank account.

This doesn't have to be an actual business account—it can be a regular checking account—but it should be separate from your personal bank accounts. All money you earn and expenses you have should flow in and out of this account. I recommend getting a separate savings account too so that you can put aside the money you'll need for taxes and other big expenses. There are lots of options for low- or no-fee accounts, and some are targeted towards freelancers and solo businesses, so look around and see what makes sense for you.

After you've been around for a while or have a certain level of business, it may make sense to get an actual business account. These often come with perks—I get cash back on certain types of purchases each month and a cool automatic check deposit machine with mine. Many have options for a business line of credit. Again, look around and see what makes the most sense for you in terms of money limits, fees, etc.

Get a business credit card.

Get a separate credit card for your business too. It doesn't have to be a fancy business account, just a separate card that's used only for business. Why?

1. It keeps your business and personal purchases separate, so that you don't have to spend time at the end of every month going through your statement to figure out which is which.
2. If you're using a debit card or paying for all of your online business expenses directly from your bank account, you always need to make sure you have the cash on hand to cover those expenses in advance. What happens when money is tight or you need something big and unexpected?
3. Credit cards offer all kinds of rewards and actual business credit card accounts usually offer even more. I have a small business credit card through my bank that gives me extra cash rewards on typical business purchases (like office supplies), and my previous card gave me more airline miles per purchase than my personal credit card.

TAKE THE
Next Step

GOOD

☐ Open a checking account for your business.
☐ Get a separate credit card for the business.

BETTER

☐ Open a savings account for your business and sock away extra money for taxes and unexpected expenses.
☐ Apply for an EIN.

BEST

☐ Hire an accountant and bookkeeper. Ask for advice about insurance and business structure.

Brainstorm your brand.

Your brand is more than just your logo or the look of your website—it's the way you present yourself to the world *and* the way the world perceives you. Some of that is under your control, and some of it isn't. Your brand will evolve over time as clients work with you and form their own opinions of the experience—and as you evolve and change.

So spend some time thinking about how you want to present yourself and how you want potential clients to perceive you. Think about the ideal client and target market—your brand should match that. For example, if you're targeting high-end financial planners, then a DIY logo in a cartoonish font or using a lot of informal slang on your website isn't going to inspire confidence that you can provide the services they need. How your business looks and what you say should resonate with your audience. That doesn't mean that you can't be yourself or have flexibility in your style or messaging, but you should always keep in mind your potential client and what they're looking for.

As you develop and refine your brand, consider these questions.

- What key words do you want customers to think of when they think of you?
- Why are you in business? What problems are you trying to solve?
- How do you want people to feel when they work with you?
- How would you describe your personality? How would people who know you describe your personality?
- What are your core values? Do you have a mission statement?

Pick a name

What will you call your new enterprise? If it's just you, it can be as simple as Jane Smith Designs, and you're off and running. If the business is bigger than you, you'll want to spend more time coming up with ideas. The name you choose should reflect your business's identity and goals and will help you market. The name will hopefully be with you for a long time, and it can be expensive to get it registered and printed on promotional materials, so it's worth thinking through carefully.

In my first year of part-time freelancing, I called myself Amy Weiher Design. That felt really boring to me, and it didn't reflect the kind of first impression I wanted people to have. I made lists of possible names that had anything to do with graphic design, my favorite number, attributes I wanted to be known for, where I lived, and nothing resonated. I don't quite remember when I stumbled upon Weiher Creative (pronounced "we're creative"), but it was a total "well, duh!" moment for me.

Graphic designer Sarah Spoelstra wishes she could say her business name had something to do with design, but it doesn't. "I wanted a name that felt like home to me and gave a glimpse of my personality. My happy place is near the small town of Rochford in the Black Hills of South Dakota. Population twenty-five. Back when I was a kid, it had a general store, bar, and church. (Pretty much all the essentials.) What I loved about Rochford was how the town represented the blue collar, hardworking, somewhat rebellious folks of my home state. I felt like I could identify with that. So, the name for my business—Moonshine Design—was inspired by the bar in town: Moonshine Gulch Saloon."

Here are a few more things to think about.

- Make sure the name you choose is different from your competitors. Even if they don't accuse you of trademark infringement, you want a name that sets you apart from the competition. Being confused with a competing business is never a good thing.
- Choose a name that people can spell and pronounce.
- Try to choose a name that is unique and creative and still reflects your business. What do you want to be known for? What imagery do you want customers to think of when they hear your business name?
- Don't be too specific, especially if you think you might expand your offerings later on or move to a new location.
- Get opinions from others in your industry and people in your target market.
- If you're forming a business entity (LLC or corporation), you might be required to include that as part of your name (refer back to the previous chapter). Your state may also have a list of verbiage that you're not allowed to use if you're not in a specific industry. Start by visiting the main government website for your state and see what resources are available (the state of Washington, as an example, has an entire sub-website dedicated to small business guidance with a ton of information).

Before you commit to anything, research your state's legal guidelines via your state website or state Secretary of State to be sure the name isn't being used by someone else. Do a search through the United States Patent and Trademark Office to see what names are already registered, and do a quick search to see what else pops up that might not be formally registered. You might even want to talk to a trademark attorney to find out whether your name is eligible to be trademarked. Teresa Torres of Product Talk wishes she had done that. "I'm not able to trademark 'Product Talk' (it's too generic), and it's been a huge headache. Tons of people use that name, and it causes a lot of confusion." Most attorneys will advise on this for free because they want to earn the business of doing the filing.

Can't I just use my own name?

Sure, but it's worth considering a few things first.

Your name is you (obviously), and if your company has the same name, then the company is also you, and it can be really hard to separate the two (both from a client perspective and from your own view). What happens as you grow and get employees? Will there be a disconnect when clients are hiring you (or what they think is you) and then find themselves talking to or working with a different person?

Posting online becomes a bit trickier. Are you posting as you personally or as your company, and can people tell the difference? Do you need to be more careful about what you say, like, or share?

What happens if you decide to sell the business down the road? It's easier to separate the value of the business versus the value of your individual brand if the business isn't named after you.

None of that needs to be a deal-breaker or a reason not to use your name, but these are things to consider.

Get a logo

This isn't critical up front depending on what you're doing (the designer in me is cringing right now). Let's be real—branding done properly is expensive and hard to afford when you're just starting out. I get it. Other designers might argue with me on this, but I believe that if you're a solopreneur or small business you can get by for now with a quickie logo done on the cheap and do proper branding once you're more established and have the money to upgrade. If you're starting a larger enterprise, like an agency or a higher-end boutique consulting business, you need to have strong branding up front.

Going into detail about the dos and don'ts of logos and branding could fill an entire book, but I've listed some guidelines below, and you can download a handy checklist on my website: goodworkbook.com. These recommendations assume that you're not a graphics expert, so my fellow designers can skip this part.

- **Keep it simple.** Your logo doesn't have to convey every aspect of what you do at a glance. Some of the most well-known logos, like the Nike swoosh, are really simple and don't literally convey much at all in the graphic itself, other than a feeling or hint at what they do. Depending on your business, and especially as you're getting started, there's nothing wrong with just typesetting your name in a nice font and letting your supporting graphics do the talking about what you do.
- **Be careful about using stock illustrations (clip art).** Depending on the source, you may not legally be allowed to use it in a logo, so check any image usage rules before you commit. Even if it is OK to use, keep in mind that if you found it and downloaded it, other people likely have too.
- **Keep it readable.** Some fonts are harder to read than others, and trying to turn a letter or two into a graphic can make the name confusing or hard to read. Get feedback from a few other people who don't already know your business name to see if they can understand it.
- **Make sure you're not inadvertently including imagery that is sexual or inappropriate (unless that's what you're going for).** Share it with people to make sure they aren't seeing something you missed.
- **Watch your tone.** If you're starting a copywriting firm that specializes in the funeral industry, you don't want to use fonts or images that are silly or fun. That doesn't mean that you can't or shouldn't add any personality to your logo, but it should feel appropriate for the situation.

If you've read the previous five tips and your head is spinning, or if you have no desire to try and create a logo yourself, fear not—there are lots of ways to get help. If you have the money or are offering a higher-end service, a graphic designer can help you. The easiest ways to find a designer are to do a search for graphic designers in your area or to ask colleagues for recommendations. If you're looking for help that is quick and cheap, there are lots of services like fiverr.com, upwork.com, and 99designs.com where you can get cheap logos fast. The quality isn't always great and you likely won't have access to all of the final logo files that a proper design firm would provide, but it can at least get you something to start with.

If you're set on doing it yourself but don't have the design know-how, consider using a program like Canva or Adobe Express. Both of these online programs have a library of available fonts and images that you can use to create a logo for yourself. But keep in mind that the images are stock illustrations that other users have access to as well, so it's quite possible that other people will have the same logo as you.

Consider your branding

You can make a positive first impression—even on a shoestring budget—with consistent branding. Your materials, including printed pieces, website, signage, digital graphics, slide decks, should have:

- **Matching logo on all materials.** Use the same logo everywhere so that it's recognizable.
- **Matching fonts.** Pick two fonts that you like that look good together and only use those as much as possible. Feel free to sprinkle in the occasional new font for things like headlines or callout text, but in general you should use the same fonts on everything.
- **Matching colors.** Choose two to three colors that you like that give the right vibe for your business and stick to those. Have another accent color or two that you like that can be used sparingly for special occasions. As an example, if your company colors are midnight blue and teal, maybe your accent color is a bright orange that is only used for things like website buttons or your call to action headlines.
- **Consistent organization name everywhere, including how it's capitalized and punctuated.** If your design firm is named JP Designs, make sure that's how you spell it everywhere. If it's one way on your website and "J P Designs" on your email, it's confusing. I do quite a bit of work with shopping centers, and sometimes the tenant names will be listed one way in one place (Molly's) and a different name elsewhere (mollys). Figure out how you want to be known and stick to it.
- **Similar types of photos/photo treatments and illustrations throughout**. Images on your website and promotional materials should match. If you're using cute cartoon icons in one place, use that same style everywhere. If you're showcasing your services with large black and white photographs, then the rest of the images on your site should also be black and white.
- **Crisp, clear images.** Blurry images give a less than stellar impression—definitely not how you want to sell your services. There are lots of places to find good stock photography—my go-to sites are iStockphoto, Shutterstock, Pexels, and Unsplash for free or low-cost photos that look great. I recommend buying the largest file size you can.
- **Same look and feel on all materials.** Using the same fonts and coloring on everything will help your customers recognize you and know at a glance that they're in the right place. If you are in an industry that is

bright and fun, then be bright and fun everywhere. If you're doing something more serious, then that feeling should be conveyed on all of your marketing. In addition, find or create templates for invoices, proposals, and any other documents you'll use regularly and stick with them. Templates will save you time and ensure a consistent look.

- **Same tone of voice in your writing.** Whether your information is presented in a serious way with lots of industry jargon or in a more friendly way with jokes and lighthearted comments, be consistent. It should sound like the same person is talking no matter where the writing is.
- **Consistent message and call to action.** You should generally be telling people the same message and asking them to do the same thing— hire you to refresh their brand or write their case studies, take your content-creation course, or sign up for your free consultation. Repetition is your friend!
- **Consistently well-designed materials.** Even if you don't have the money to hire a designer, employing the tips above will go a long way to making you look professional. Even if you're the best in your field, poorly designed materials reflect poorly on you.

If you don't have the time or know-how to do all this yourself, it's worth the money to hire a professional. They can set you up with introductory materials and principles that you can implement as you go. If you can't afford to get help, programs like Canva and Adobe Express have easy-to-update templates for projects of all types. If you're a little more design-program savvy, sites like Creative Market, Shutterstock, iStock, and Stock Layouts have lots of different types of templates that you can purchase and update. But with any of these options, keep in mind that they are templates available to everyone, and it's likely that you'll come across the same designs being used by other organizations at some point. I use Canva to create quick graphics for our PTA events at my son's school, and I regularly see the same designs being used by other local PTAs too. Not a big deal in that scenario, but less than ideal in a business situation where you're trying to sell yourself as a unique service provider.

Set up a business website or at least an email address

Your website is the first place many potential clients will encounter you. Depending on what you do, you may not need a website when you start your business (the designer in me cringed when I wrote that). But as a creative service, I recommend at least having some sort of basic online presence and an email address associated with your business—potential clients will want to see samples of the work that you've done before they hire you. Even if you've never had an actual client, write some sample blog posts or design some personal projects so that it looks like you have some experience. Even a simple page that tells a bit about you and what you do with a link to Behance or some other portfolio site is better than nothing.

As someone who routinely looks for contract help, I'm really hesitant to reach out to anyone that doesn't have their own email address and website unless they are a referral. My dad runs a really successful consulting business and did so for twenty years with an AOL address and no website, so it's possible but times have changed. Given how much of our time is spent online and people's general hesitancy to make a phone call rather than send a text or email, it's a lot harder for customers to find you organically without some sort of digital presence. If they can't find you through a search or contact you electronically, they likely won't find you or contact you at all.

Unless you're selling something that requires an online store, a really simple single-page website is all you need to get started. It should have a few basic types of information on it

- What you do (your services).
- Who you do it for (your target customers).
- Your value proposition (why should someone hire you?).
- Who you are.
- Project samples.
- Contact information.

If you can afford it, and if wordsmithing isn't your thing, it's worth hiring a copywriter to help you. There are tons of do-it-yourself design options out there for cheap, so even if you don't have a clue about how to code a website, it's easy to do. Once you're established, you can do something more complex.

Want to make your own website?

These days it's really easy to set up a website, even if you don't have any coding knowledge (or any interest in learning). Listed below are some good options for basic websites and a few pros and cons of each. This is by no means an exhaustive list, but it gives you a look at some of the bigger options out there.

✓ **Wix (wix.com).** Wix has hundreds of customizable drag and drop website templates and a library of free photos and icons that use can use. Wix templates are unstructured, meaning that website elements can be placed anywhere, giving you more freedom to customize the layouts (which could be a good thing or a bad thing depending on your visual skills). The sites are hosted on Wix's servers, so there's no need to install software or buy hosting, and the monthly fees are pretty low. They've been around for a while and have a very large userbase, so they're not likely to fold any time soon. The main argument against using Wix? Your site can only live on the Wix platform, and once you go live, that's it. If you lose access to your account, decide you want to switch to a different hosting company, or switch to a new site template, you'll need to start over from scratch. Wix sites tend to be slower and aren't fully responsive either, so your site might look a little odd on phones and tablets.

✓ **Squarespace (squarespace.com).** Squarespace is also a hosted website solution (no software to install or additional hosting needed) with a huge range of Adobe and Google fonts included, access to the entire Unsplash image library, and options for inexpensive Getty images—a big plus for designers. Templates are easy to edit and tend to be a bit more modern and clean, so designers and artists tend to prefer them. Unlike Wix, templates are structured, meaning that website elements snap into columns and grids, which may make it easier for non-designers to make a clean, appealing site. They're also fully responsive and automatically scale for tablets and mobile devices, which is great for accessibility and search engine optimization (SEO). The main argument against Squarespace? Since the site lives on their server, if change your mind about the design or the hosting, you have to start all over again.

✓ **Shopify (shopify.com).** Shopify is user-friendly e-commerce platform for small businesses who want to set up an online store and sell online through one streamlined dashboard. Unlike other hosted options, Shopify prioritizes selling products rather than conveying information. Both Wix and Squarespace do offer e-commerce add-ons, but it's not their primary focus. Shopify has fewer templates and a higher initial price point, but if you're selling products, Shopify is the way to go.

✓ **WordPress (wordpress.com) or Webflow (webflow.com).** If you really want control over your website and want to be able to host it or move it anywhere, then WordPress or Webflow are the way to go. Both offer premade drag and drop templates (WordPress calls them themes), access to the underlying code, and the ability to host your site anywhere, and both are relatively easy to use. The main difference is that WordPress uses plug-ins for a lot of its functionality, where Webflow is self-contained. If you have access to a web developer, then either of these options is a no-brainer.

Write your elevator pitch.

How will you answer when someone asks what you do? You'll want to have a very brief statement at the ready that explains what you do and who you do it for. At first, it can be as simple as "I'm a [blank] who does [blank] for [blank]." Once you've been around for a while, you'll figure out how you can refine and jazz that up. It took me ten years to finally settle on mine: "I create graphic design for good causes and good people with good intentions." Once you've got the basics down, play with it! Try out a new pitch every time you talk to someone new at a networking event and see what resonates with people or sparks conversation.

Public speaking coach Gigi Rosenberg recommends you change up your pitch depending on who you're talking to. For example, you'll have a casual one you might use with a new neighbor and a more formal one you might use in a meeting with a client. Her top three tips are: (1) use examples so you paint a picture in the mind of your listener, (2) channel warmth as if you're talking to a friend, and (3) if it's getting too complicated, imagine you're explaining what you do to your grandpa. Regardless of what you say, practice it so that it flows off your tongue at a moment's notice. And don't worry if it's not perfect. "Your elevator speech will always be a work in progress, always evolving as you grow, the world changes, and your business matures," Rosenberg said.

TAKE THE
☑ *Next Step* ☑

GOOD

- ☐ Decide on a company name.
- ☐ Write a simple elevator pitch for your business.

BETTER

- ☐ Set up a basic online presence, even if it's just one page with some portfolio samples and contact information.

BEST

- ☐ Design a logo and a more robust website presence. Make adjustments as you continue to grow and hone your brand message and area of expertise.
- ☐ Update your elevator pitch as you get clearer on your business focus.

Consider your collateral.

Don't get caught up in thinking that you have to have a full suite of fancy promotional materials right off the bat. I fell into that trap, and I've had a big batch of pocket folders collecting dust in a cabinet for nineteen years that I will likely never use, along with envelopes in every size and color that I thought were cool and would eventually do something with. Spoiler alert, I haven't. Don't spend money on supplies unless you'll actually use them. Then go for it.

The fact that most business is done online these days makes it really easy and a lot less expensive to get started with the basics. When you're first starting out, you probably don't need much. A business card, envelope, and digital letterhead will do the trick. If you have the funding, a thank you card is great to have too. Other than that, you'll need some sort of estimate sheet and a proposal document. Make a template so that you can easily update or duplicate it every time a new project comes along—hopefully, you'll need to use it a lot! You'll also need a good contract (see the "Use a Contract" chapter in the next section). If you'll be active on social media, you may want to create image templates that you can update and use repeatedly.

Need help creating these documents? Online programs like FreshBooks and QuickBooks have easy templates for estimates and invoices, along with the bookkeeping services they offer. Design sites like Canva and Adobe Express also have templates that you can modify, and even Word has basic templates that you can edit. Proposal templates vary more widely and tend to be a lot more customized, but you can find examples online via a quick search, and you can purchase templates to modify on sites like Shutterstock, iStock, and Creative Market. The best way I've found to improve my materials over the years is to see what my colleagues and competitors are using and make adjustments to mine based on what others do well. People in my creative groups tend to be pretty generous when it comes to sharing best practices and sample documents, so don't be afraid to ask!

It's also a great idea to have some sort of slide deck or one-sheet that highlights your capabilities and gives some information about the services you offer, who your target markets are, and samples of your work. Something that is easy to email to people who want more information is great, and you can post it on your website for easy downloading too. I created a basic template for myself, so when a new prospect asks to see some samples of a particular type of project or niche, it's easy to swap out a few images and send it off.

As you grow and get into the groove of who you are as a business, you can start adding in fancy mailers, giveaways, and other cool printed items.

TAKE THE
Next Step

GOOD

☐ Get a business card and digital letterhead.

BETTER

☐ Create an estimate form and invoice form that you can easily duplicate. If you're using an online company for estimating or invoicing, personalize their template with your logo.

BEST

☐ Create a slide deck or one-pager that showcases your capabilities and sample work.

Get over jealousy.

I can't count the number of times I've looked at another website or seen a project from another designer and thought, "I wish I'd done that," or "I wish I had that client or type of project," or "I wish I was that good or had that style." Especially in creative fields, jealousy and insecurity comes with the territory. There will always be someone "better" or "more talented" than you (and that's a relative term). There will always be someone else who has bigger and better projects or who gets to work with your dream client. It's easy to feel deflated.

But instead of letting it defeat you, let it motivate or inspire you. If there's a type of client or project you want, chase after it. Figure out what you need to learn or do or who you need to connect with to make that happen. See a cool feature on another website that you wish you had thought of? Find a way to make your own unique version of it. The contact form on my website was born that way—I saw something similar but much shorter on another site, loved the concept, and then reworked and rewrote it to fit what I needed.

Also keep these things in mind.

1. We all have different ways of doing things, none of which are wrong (OK, some of them are). In a creative field, your style of design or writing or coding will be different from the person next to you. If you're the brains behind the operation, your strategy will be different from the thinking and solutions of your competitors. As long as you're getting the job done and clients are happy, do what works for you.
2. You bring a specific skill set to the table, and the person you're jealous of can't necessarily do what you do. I have a colleague who is an amazing designer—I love everything she creates and am insanely jealous whenever I see a completed project. I would kill to be able to say that her work was mine. And yet, her style would not work for any of my clients—clients who love what I do and keep coming back for more. I can't do what she does, at least not without a ton of effort, and she can't do what I do. And there's room for both of us.
3. You never really know what is happening behind the scenes for anyone else. That project you think is amazing might have been done for the worst client ever. Maybe the copywriter you're admiring had someone else write that article that you love.
4. Someone else is likely jealous of you too! No matter what you're doing, there is always someone else in the world who would do anything to be in your place or have what you have.

Whenever I feel myself getting jealous of someone, I try to put it in perspective. If there's something I can learn from it, I do. If it just means that I'm gonna be jealous for a while, so be it. Stick to being the best *you* possible, not a worse someone else.

TAKE THE Next Step

GOOD

☐ When you feel jealous of someone else, use it as motivation or inspiration.

BETTER

☐ Find something to learn from the people and work you admire.

BEST

☐ Remember that you bring a very specific skill set to the table, and no one else can do what you do in exactly the same way.

THE BEST TIME TO PLANT A TREE WAS 20 YEARS AGO. THE SECOND BEST TIME IS NOW.

— UNKNOWN

The key is to take the first step. You don't even have to dive in—if dipping a toe in and moving really slowly feels better, then do that. Then do the next thing. And the next. Before you know it, you'll be chugging along nicely.

FIND A GOOD RHYTHM

Set your personal boundaries and expectations.

Part of setting expectations is setting boundaries—and sticking to them. Full disclosure: I struggle with this. A lot. But I'm much better at it now than I used to be.

You set your own rules, even if that means choosing to accept the terms set by your client. Once you've set boundaries for yourself and have set expectations with your customers, keep them. Keep them even if clients balk and it's uncomfortable. Otherwise, they're nothing more than wishes in the wind, and clients will learn that you'll do whatever they want. That's not good. You'll be miserable. After a while, if you decide to change them, you have every right to do that and be sure to update expectations with people who need to know.

As you decide what your business looks like, here are some things to think about. We've already touched on some of these in the first section, but it helps to think about them in terms of boundaries as a whole too.

- When do you work?
    - → What hours are you in the office?
    - → What days are you in the office?
    - → Are you available on weekends?
    - → Will you work nights or early mornings?
    - → What days or times of the week will you block off for yourself or your family?
    - → What will you say if someone wants something outside of your work hours?
    - → Are you willing to make exceptions for certain clients? Which or what kind of clients? Will you charge higher fees for this time?
- How can clients reach you?
    - → Will you answer your phone and email all day long, or will you block out specific times for responding?
    - → Can clients text you?
    - → Will you respond to emails and phone calls during your off hours or on weekends?
    - → Will you connect to clients on social media and respond to them there?
    - → Will you have separate work and personal phones?
    - → What will you do if someone contacts you in a different way than you prefer or isn't respectful of your communication styles/boundaries?
    - → Are you willing to make exceptions for certain clients? Which or what kind of clients? Will you charge higher fees for this time?
- How will you work?
    - → Will you send everything via email? Will you talk through most things on the phone?
    - → Do you need focused time to get project work done? Can you be interrupted—by whom and how often?
    - → Where will you work?
    - → Can customers pop in (in person or via phone) or do they need an appointment?
    - → Will you use a customer relationship management (CRM) or project management software (like Asana, Basecamp, or Trello) to keep track of people and projects?
    - → How will you track your time?

- What sort of paperwork and contracts will you use?
  - → How will you prepare and send estimates?
  - → When will you require a deposit—every project, big projects, new clients?
  - → Will you charge rush fees? When and how much?
  - → How will you prepare and send invoices?
  - → What are your payment terms (due on receipt, net 30, etc.)? Many large companies dictate their own payment terms, and they're often longer than thirty days. Are you willing to accept those terms?
  - → Will you offer discounts for early payment? How much?
  - → Will you charge late fees on invoices? How much?
  - → How can customers pay you? Will you cover any fees for credit card or bank transfers, or will they?
  - → If a client asks you to sign a nondisclosure agreement (NDA), will you?
- What will you do when things go wrong?
  - → What if a prospect won't sign your contract?
  - → What if a client won't pay?
  - → What if a client is late or doesn't provide their materials? What if they don't stick to the schedule?
  - → What happens when clients start asking for more than you originally agreed upon (commonly known as *scope creep*)? When will you do a change order?
  - → What if the project is killed or delayed indefinitely?
  - → What will you do if there are printing or fabrication errors or supply chain issues that delay parts and materials?
  - → Will you accept rush projects or off-hours work? What will you charge for that?
  - → What if a client is unhappy with the work you're doing or did on a project?
  - → How will you decide when a client or vendor needs to be fired?
  - → How will you handle conflicts when there is conflicting feedback from different people at a company?
- Will you work with contractors for associated services?
  - → Where will you find them?
  - → Will you hire them by project or on retainer?
  - → Do they need to sign an NDA?
  - → Will you pay them when they invoice you or after the client pays you?
  - → Will contractors work directly with your clients or go through you?

You may not have all of the answers to these questions yet, and that's OK. But if you're at least aware of them, you'll be more prepared to decide how to respond when they do arise—because they will.

If you want to violate a boundary in a specific instance, do so consciously. And let the person on the receiving end know that you're making an exception so that it's clear. For example, I don't work nights or weekends (or at least I don't tell clients when I do). A few months ago, I designed a report and corresponding slide deck full of charts and graphs for a client to present at a Saturday morning conference. We knew in advance that there would likely be data changes up until the last minute, and the final PDF and slides were approved at 11 p.m. on Friday night. I had made it clear in advance that I was going to make that time available to them, so they were aware that I was making an exception to my usual schedule. When I sent the final approved files to them, despite the fact that I was exhausted and really wanted to be done with the project, I told them that if any last-second adjustments need-ed to be made before they went on stage, they could text me overnight and I would get up early to get them done. Sure enough, a text came through at 3:15 a.m. asking me if I could adjust one chart (and apologizing profusely), so I got up at 7 a.m. and edited the chart, shipped it off, and went back to bed.

Why did I agree to go out of my way like that? A few reasons. The presen-tation was the result of several months of work on a report I was really proud of and I wanted it to be done right. The project was done for a new client that I wanted to work with again, so going a bit out of my way made me stand out and set the expectation that I'm someone who will do a great job and can be counted on to do it right. The project was also the kind that I want more of, so I can now use it in my portfolio and as a case study. The next time that client writes a similar report or has colleagues who do, they're more likely to refer me. Would I do that every weekend? Hell no. Did I wonder if I was setting an unsustainable precedent with a new client? Not really. In this in-stance I was clear that I was making an exception for them outside of my usual schedule, and Saturday morning conferences aren't very common. If they do come back and need another early-morning delivery, I can decide what to do. Deliberately choosing when to go above and beyond has paid off for me over the years.

TAKE THE Next Step

GOOD

☐ Think through your answers to the questions above. Write a set of basic ground rules that you will ask clients to follow.

BETTER

☐ Think through some scenarios in which you will refuse to break your boundaries, and have scripts ready so you can respond.

BEST

☐ Include a list of basic expectations in your proposals and on your website. Talk through them with clients so you're all on the same page.

Act like a professional.

Freelancers sometimes have a less than stellar reputation. The word I hear most to describe them is *flaky*. (See also *irresponsible, unreliable.*) Ugh. Don't be the freelancer who gives that stereotype legs.

Even if it's just you in your sweatpants at a laptop on your kitchen table, you're a business. And clients don't need to know about the sweatpants. Act like a professional and clients will treat you that way (i.e. give you more business). In general, this means letting people know what to expect from you, and then following up on it (this includes using a contract, which is so important that we'll cover it separately in the next section).

Have a set-ish schedule.

People generally want to be able to reach you during working hours. That doesn't mean you always need to be available from 9 a.m. to 5 p.m., although that helped me establish credibility when I first started out. But let your customers know what to expect. If working early in the morning and again later in the day is what works for you, say so, and then be available during that time—*available* is the key word here; clients want to be able to connect with you easily and reliably. If clients have to guess when you'll be around, eventually they'll stop guessing and go elsewhere for more stability.

My friend Teresa dropped a hairdresser that she loved for this very reason. "The only way to schedule an appointment was to text her. That's fine. But she would often go days before responding. Since she didn't publish her availability anywhere, we always had to go back and forth several times, and she would often go days in between texts. It would take weeks to schedule an appointment. Who needs that?"

Respond to emails in a reasonable amount of time.

It doesn't have to be immediately but hopefully within twenty-four hours, depending on the type of business you're running and the kinds of requests you get from customers. If you can't respond quickly, set up an autoresponder telling the recipient when you will get back to them so they don't feel ignored. Don't wait days to respond to something unless that's what you've told them to expect.

Answer the phone.

Or set a precedent that you won't answer the phone but will return calls as promptly as you can. I didn't have a fancy smartphone when I first started out, so I answered every call. Nowadays my iPhone either tells me that a number is spam or guesses at who it is as it cross-references numbers in my emails, so I can be more selective about when I answer the phone.

With so many other means of quick communication these days (IM, Slack, Zoom, email, Teams, texting, chat, etc.), the phone isn't necessarily king for most of us these days. The tricky part here, as with any of the other communication channels above, is that a ringing phone or chiming app can be an unwelcome interruption, especially if you're in the middle of focused work, in the creative flow, or doing critical thinking. Whether you answer it or not, the damage is already done, so consider reclaiming some control over your devices by turning off apps or notifications when you need to focus, and then checking them again at regular intervals. Most apps have some sort of away setting so the message sender knows what to expect. If you're the one doing the sending, you can help cut down on Slack and IM notifications by consolidating your thoughts into a single message, using threads for responses, replacing follow-up messages with emojis when possible, and generally setting expectations around how you'll communicate with each other.

Do what you say you're going to do.

If you tell a customer you'll check in with them at 3 p.m. on Monday, then check in with them at 3 p.m. on Monday. If you are contracted to provide three different designs on a poster, then provide all three. If the client is expecting a proposal in fifteen parts, then get all fifteen parts done and sent. If there's something you can't or won't do, don't say you will. If they ask for something you can't or won't do, say no.

Meet deadlines.

If that client is expecting their fifteen-part proposal by end of day Thursday, then get it to them by end of day Thursday. Better yet, get it to them by lunchtime. Or even on Wednesday. You don't need to go overboard here (see the chapter "Be wary of 'underpromise and overdeliver'"), but you do need to be realistic when setting deadlines of your own or agreeing to deadlines set by the client.

What does it mean to be realistic? That depends. Ask yourself these questions.

- What time commitment is needed to complete the requested task? Is that time variable and adjustable (like with a creative project) or is it a fixed amount of time, like the time it takes to print or fabricate something?
- What does your schedule currently look like? Do you have meetings or other appointments that will eat into your work time, or is your schedule open at the moment? What other projects do you have on your plate?
- Is the client asking for a specific deadline, or is there flexibility to set your own delivery date?
- How are you feeling physically? If you're dealing with a health issue, even a small, temporary one, do you have the physical capability to add this to your plate right now, or do you need to add more time?
- How are you feeling mentally? Are you energized and on a roll, or are you dealing with some burnout or depression that might slow you down?
- What is it like to work with this client? Are they easy to work with or will they micromanage you and require extra time for meetings or other communication?
- Are there other family or personal commitments that you should consider? Will you have the time to do the job and still fulfill your nonwork obligations without making yourself crazy?
- How challenging is the project? Will it require a lot of thought, mental energy, and focus, or is it something that's easy for you to do and needs little effort on your part?
- Can you get outside help? Do you need it?
- Are the effort and time worth the money?
- If the answers to some of the questions above mean that taking on the project might mean working longer hours, more stress, or saying no to something in your personal life, is there still a valid reason to consider saying yes to it?

Being professional also doesn't mean that you'll be perfect all the time. Shit happens. Kids get sick, computers crash, and car accidents happen at lunch (yup, been there). Or maybe you underestimated how much time something would take. For those of us in creative fields, sometimes inspiration doesn't strike when you need it to. When shit happens, it's perfectly reasonable to reach out to your client, explain what happened and why you need more time, and then tell them what you can do. They may say no, and you may just have to suck it up and rush something through, but at least you're communicating *so they know what to expect*. That's really what it's all about. The worst thing you can do is just ignore the deadline and go MIA. That's a great way to see your clients go MIA too.

Handle rejection.

If you're anything like me, this can be a tough lesson to learn—and learn again. But you are not your work or your business, and decisions that clients make usually have nothing to do with you. It's their job to ask you to do more work for less money—they're not doing it to annoy you or because they don't like you.

If you don't win a project or make a sale, it likely has nothing to do with you—and you can ask what that reason is so that you can grow from it. When I lose a project to another designer, I congratulate the client on making the decision that they feel is best for them, express my disappointment that it isn't me, and then ask if there was something in particular that took me out of the running. I don't always get an answer, but sometimes I do, and the answers are the same—it was either due to price, a change in strategy at the company, or a previous existing relationship. Nothing to do with me personally. I let them know that if their chosen option doesn't work out or if something comes along that would be a better fit for me, I'm here and interested.

If you're like me, the work you do is a huge part of who you are. You feel passionate about it, want to learn and get better at it, and share what you know with the world (for money). So when a prospect doesn't want to work with you, a customer doesn't like the solution you provided, or a client fires you, it feels like a personal rejection. But it's not. You are more than just a [insert your job title here]. Zoom out and remember all the other roles and interests that you find meaningful.

TAKE THE Next Step

GOOD

☐ Decide how and when you'll communicate and stick to it.

BETTER

☐ Set realistic deadlines and then stick to them.
☐ If you don't know why you lost out on a project, ask.

BEST

☐ When you're going to deviate from the usual schedule or see an issue coming up, let people know. Be proactive.

NOTES

Use a contract.

Diamonds are a girl's best friend, unless she runs her own business, in which case her BFF is a contract. It's the most important business document you'll need—and need often.

Contracts can be intimidating. They're usually filled with legal jargon that doesn't make sense to regular people. They can also feel cold and impersonal—total vibe killer. I remember hiring a contractor to do work for me many years ago, and we had a lovely conversation about the great work we were going to do together. She sent me a contract to sign, and it was so complicated and full of legalese that I suddenly felt like I was talking to someone else who had built a brick wall between us. Even though the actual text of the contract was reasonable, it left a bit of a sour taste in my mouth. I don't want any of my clients to feel that way when they get paperwork from me, so I hesitated to use a contract for many years. I designed an estimate form that included a few contract-like lines about payment and cancellation policies, but otherwise didn't use an actual contract unless someone sent one to me.

It wasn't until I met a lawyer who talked like a real human being that I discovered that contracts don't have to be scary. They really can be written in plain English, in a conversational tone, with the occasional necessary legal term thrown in. It was truly eye-opening to me to realize that business paperwork could be written that way, and it has changed how I speak on my other forms as well.

My contract essentially says that my client and I are a team, and I will do my part and they will do their part, and here's what happens if something goes sideways. It incorporates some of my branding and voice, like using "Yawn" as the header for some of the more boring sections, so overall it feels like a part of the conversation we're having rather than some lawyer in a suit taking over us.

I no longer see a contract as a set of handcuffs but as a magical protective cloak that covers both you and the client. Almost like a prenup, it should detail clearly what you will do, what they will do, how you'll do it, what is expected, and what you will do if something goes wrong. It's all about establishing a clear, mutually beneficial agreement—and covering your ass.

Mark Grimm is a professional speaker and speaking coach who has negotiated scores of contracts between his twelve-year television anchor career, book writing, and twenty years in business. "Don't settle for a bunch of legalese just because they say it's standard language. Insist on plain language so everyone understands what the deal is. Be clear on the steps necessary if one side wants out. What is required from both sides? Be clear about the purpose of the contract. How does each side benefit? Are there any specific reasons the contract could be voided during the term? Nail this down with specifics, whether that includes some sort of morality clause (which is too vague) or politically incorrect speech. A contract should also include a statement on your freedom once the contract expires. Are you free to work for a competitor right away?"

Here are the basic things a contract should include.

- **Who.** Your full legal business name and the client's full business name. It should also spell out who the main points of contact will be for both organizations.
- **What.** The scope of work should be clearly defined, in as much detail as possible. Here's what you are hiring me to do, and here's what I need you to do or provide in order to make that happen. List anything that is not included in the scope, whether it's being provided to you by the client or isn't expected to be needed. You might also include a list of additional services that could potentially be added to the project and at what cost as an attachment. The list might end up getting you some extra work that the client may not have previously considered, and it won't require the need for a new contract.
- **When.** Outline the project schedule, with due dates and turnaround times for your part of the work, and specify any client related dates too. Spell out any consequences that might occur if those due dates aren't met at any point. Deadlines are a two-way street, so make sure the client is clear on what they need to do to help the project succeed.
- **Payment.** The contract should clearly spell out all of the project fees and payment schedules. Outline any extra costs, like stock photography or printing. If the client doesn't make a payment on time, specify what happens next in terms of interest, late fees, and work stoppage. If the client disappears for a month, what happens?
- **Final deliverables.** Outline what is considered a final deliverable—the final thing that they own the copyright to once the invoice is paid. Outline what isn't included, like initial drafts or concepts that you own the copyright to. Specify what you can use in your portfolio or share online for promotion and how you'll credit that. Promise that whatever you create will actually be created by you (no generative AI), so that you can legally transfer the copyright.
- **Termination.** Either you or the client has the right to end the project at any point. If the client wants to terminate the contract, what fees will you impose? What conversations need to be had in advance to try and fix the problem? What will you give them or do if you are the one to initiate the break?

- **Confidentiality, jurisdiction, and indemnification.** How will you handle confidential information, either yours or theirs? In the event that something goes catastrophically awry, where will any legal action take place? Do you need an indemnity clause to protect yourself?
- **An expiration date.** Contracts shouldn't last forever. Set an expiration date so you won't be held to old pricing or outdated information.

Finding a lawyer who will create a contract for you in plain English can be tricky, but they do exist. If you don't have the money for that, there are lots of free contract templates online that can get you started—check out the AIGA, the Freelancers Union, and the Graphic Artists Guild for resources. Even if you use a modified template, it's not a bad idea to have a lawyer review it before you use it, just to make sure you're covered.

Lauren Razzano of Digitally Driven LLC is a social media and digital marketer who learned the hard way to always use your own contracts, and when the client insists on using theirs, make sure to have an attorney look it over so there is no place for any misinterpretation. "I had a regular client insist we use their contract for a new project, and I signed it without my attorney's input because we had a relationship and I trusted them. This came back to bite me to the tune of $7,500 they didn't end up paying me (during the pandemic) after work was completed. When my attorney checked their contract he said the language was so loose that there could be a case made, but a judge would likely rule in favor of the contract author."

Once you have a contract, use it with every client, and make sure both parties understand what it says, even if it seems obvious. There's no better way to outline the expectations and consequences in advance for both of you and take the guesswork out of what to do if things don't go as planned.

TAKE THE
Next Step

GOOD

☐ Find a contract template online and modify it.

BETTER

☐ Hire a lawyer with experience in the creative services industry to review your existing contract.

BEST

☐ Hire a lawyer to write a contract for you in plain English.

Be personal.

Being professional doesn't mean that you can't be personal. You're not a robot, and most people don't want to work with a robot. I've been fortunate to work with some really lovely people for a very long time, and I think part of the reason they keep coming back is because I'm nice to work with. We're friendly and I know a little bit about their kids and hobbies. I've even met a few of them for lunch.

After my son was born, I fell into the working mom trap where I felt a lot of pressure to do it all and make sure clients knew that I was still a professional—I wouldn't let motherhood get in the way of doing my job as well as I always had. My existing clients knew that I had a baby at home, but I always felt I had to try to keep that hidden during working hours to stay "professional."

That was mentally exhausting. Even though we had full-time daycare, if I had something big scheduled, something would undoubtedly happen that required my son to be at home. I remember one day in particular: Daycare was closed and my son was home with me. It was lunchtime and I had a meeting via phone call, so I popped him in his high chair with some toys and snacks and got on my call. Every time he giggled or made any sort of noise, I panicked. *What if the client heard him? She'd think I'm not working! She'll think I'm not focused on or committed to the project we're doing!* A few minutes later, he choked on a cheese puff and projectile vomited (learning to eat is hard). I frantically tried to clean it up, keep him quiet, and have an intelligent conversation all at the same time. Luckily the call ended soon afterward, and all was well.

But I really wish I'd had the confidence to be up front about what was happening. A simple "my son is home today in case you hear any strange noises in the background" would have allowed me to be fully honest and authentic, and it might have created a better connection with the woman I was talking to. The part of my brain that was focused on panic and what-ifs could have been focused on something far more productive. But I was afraid of what people would think.

We've all got something that could potentially be a distraction, and yet we can still do our jobs—everyone has kids or pets or family or a disability or loud coworkers or neighbors who play the drums. The years of the pandemic were a game-changer for me personally, with everyone else working from home. It suddenly became normal for family, pets, and other random distractions to breach the workplace. If my son suddenly wanders into my Zoom meeting in his underpants, I can laugh about it instead of having a coronary.

Being personal doesn't mean that you should bring your kids to every meeting, make baby talk to your cat in the middle of a presentation, or spill your marital troubles to your networking group. A personal connection might be as simple as sharing a line about your favorite hobby in the last line of your bio on your website or LinkedIn profile (people will find that and connect with it!). But you can be curious about the people you're working with and be pleasant and make honest small talk. The authentic connections you make will make those working relationships more rewarding and long lasting.

The point is just to be a human being and be friendly, curious, authentic. If you're not comfortable sharing certain information about yourself, then don't. Start with a few easy, general questions and over time you might discover that you have a lot in common with the people you work with.

If you're talking to someone new, any of the usual small talk questions are fine.

- Ask how their weekend was, or if they have anything fun planned for the coming weekend.
- Ask about the weather.
- If you're on Zoom, comment on something in the room. "I love the paint color on your wall." "What a great painting you have behind you!" "Your room is so light and cheery." "What kind of plant is that?"
- In person or on Zoom, compliment something they're wearing or ask where they got the notebook they have or the stickers on their water bottle.
- A simple "How is your day going so far?" or "How are you?" can do the trick.
- And of course, it's helpful and fosters connection to respond genuinely (yet briefly) to any questions they ask.

If you're talking to someone you know better, you can get a little more personal.

- Ask about their pet.
- If they've moved to a new area, ask how the move went or how they're liking the new location.
- If they have kids, you can ask general questions like "How is your son enjoying kindergarten?" or "Do you have anything fun planned over spring break?"
- If you know they have a specific hobby or passion project, ask about that. "How is the novel coming along?" "Are you still surfing every morning?"
- Share any of the above about yourself. "I'm working from a coffee shop today because my dog got skunked last night." "I tried that new podcast

you mentioned last time and am loving it." "My son is home sick today, so if you hear cartoons in the background, it's not me!"

In general, unless you've been working with someone for a long time and know them well, keep conversations relatively surface level. What topics should you stay away from?

- **Religion.** Or at least your personal beliefs or feelings about it.
- **Physical health.** Unless someone shares something with you, it's none of your business. One of my clients recently cancelled a meeting because her daughter was in the ER as a result of an ongoing condition she has. At our rescheduled meeting, I simply said, "I hope she's doing better. That must have been scary for you!" I didn't ask what happened or what the disease is like or how often they're in the ER. And vice versa—if I'm not feeling great, I may share that with a client (especially if it's obvious that I look or sound sick). But I'm only going to share that and not go into detail about what medication I was on or how lousy I feel.
- **Mental health.** Again, if someone shares something with you, respond in a way that feels appropriate to you. "Oh, I get anxious about that too!" But don't ask about it, and don't overshare your own issues unless there's a reason to (like if you need to take some time off to deal with something).
- **Sex or personal relationships.** If a client wants to tell me that she's having a rough day because she and her husband had a fight, great. But I'm certainly not going to ask about that, nor will I share details about that part of my life. I might share stories about my husband or son if they're appropriate to the conversation we're having, but I won't share intimate details about either of them.
- **Politics.** Stay away from political discussions unless you know the other person *really* well—and maybe not even then. I have no idea how most of my clients feel about politics. I can make general assumptions based on what I do know about them, and the few that I do know came directly from things they said—not initiated by me.

TAKE THE
Next Step

GOOD

- ☐ In your next meeting, find something in the room to compliment or ask about.
- ☐ If part of your personal life intrudes into the meeting (like a dog barking at the door), acknowledge it and move on.

BETTER

- ☐ Add a bit of personality to your website and marketing materials, even if it's just a single line about a hobby or interest in your bio.

BEST

- ☐ Infuse all of your communications with a bit of your personality.

Think twice before working with family or friends.

Doing business with family and friends can be really tricky. There's a fine line between business and personal in general, even more so when the person on the other side is someone you know really well and have an emotional connection to. Throwing money into the mix adds a new layer of complexity.

I've worked with family, friends, and acquaintances over the years, and I'm always hesitant to do so, although it depends a bit on the person and the project. I designed business collateral for my father's company, and it went smoothly—he's pretty easygoing, knew enough about what he wanted to give me direction, and then trusted my expertise. I've designed logos for friends and acquaintances with lower levels of success, usually due to us not being clear up front about what we were doing and then me not getting paid and not pushing it. I have one good friend with her own consulting company who is an ongoing client, and we work really well together since she knows how both sides of a business transaction work.

Working for discounts or for free or compromising other boundaries can breed a lot of resentment in you, and you likely won't do your best work as a result, which is the opposite of what you want. You may even lose so much that you go broke, which happened to Craig. "There should be no family and friends discounts. When I started doing event planning, I thought that selling my services to family and friends at no-profit rates would easily be recovered from 'real' customers. Unfortunately, I spent so much time trying to get experience by working at those low rates that I had very little time to get real clients. For months I was struggling with very little profit, which wasn't working. When I stopped offering the discounted rate, my family and friends got angry, and I had to close my business to prevent more financial burden. I should have set the price higher from the start."

In general, I've learned to follow these rules.

- **Always use a contract, even with family.** Especially with family. Be clear on all sides about what work is being done, what it costs, and what they're responsible for. Getting the hard money conversations out of the way first helps the project go more smoothly.
- **Avoid the friends and family discount, and don't work for free.** Charge your full rate. The people who love you the most know how great you are at what you do, and they want to support you and help you succeed, so make sure that's happening financially.

- **Separate the business and the personal.** When I'm working with a friend, I like to have a clear line between our personal time and business time. The first few minutes of a meeting are spent catching up, and then we clearly state that we're entering business mode and start the business talk from there. Mixing the two conversations, at least for me, blurs the line between me as a person and the work and makes it harder for me to not take any negative feedback personally. Creating that separation helps keep us focused on the task at hand.
- **Pay attention to personalities.** If your uncle thinks he knows everything and is always right, you probably don't want to work with him. If your sister is really indecisive, you probably don't want to work with her either. They may be family, but evaluate them as you would any other potential client. If something about the way they interact with you won't allow you to do your best work, then say no. Give advice and a referral.

TAKE THE Next Step

GOOD

☐ Evaluate your potential family/friend client as you would any other prospect. Decide if you're really a good fit.

BETTER

☐ Be very clear about what work you're doing and the expectations. Talk about what could go wrong and how you'll handle any issues that come up.

BEST

☐ Provide a detailed estimate and a contract with payment terms.

Be wary of "underpromise and overdeliver."

I used to be a big fan of underpromising and overdelivering. One of my first employers would say that to us at least once a week, so it became ingrained in my psyche—always do more and do it faster.

What did that mean for me? If I promised two design directions, I did three. If I said it would be done on Wednesday, it would be done on Tuesday. If printing was involved, I would go pick it up myself and drive it to them to save the extra day for delivery. In and of themselves, none of those are that big a deal. But when you do that for every project, it adds up. To keep my pricing low, I wasn't building that extra time into my estimates, so I was essentially giving away a lot of my time and effort for free. It's no wonder I felt overworked, rushed, and burned out—*and I was doing it to myself.*

Side note: If the pressure to do more is coming from the client and not your internal monologue, that's a totally different story. See any of the chapters on boundaries and red flags.

It's a dangerous motto, and as some research is now showing, it's unnecessary. In a study published in the journal *Social Psychological and Personality Science*, University of California San Diego behavioral scientist Ayelet Gneezy and University of Chicago business professor Nicholas Epley designed a series of experiments to test whether going above and beyond paid off. The answer, surprisingly, was no. The researchers found that when the initial expectation was set, that's what the subjects focused on. As long as they received what was promised on time, nothing else really mattered.

Clients are grateful in the moment, yes. But the specific extra effort is quickly forgotten. Clients remember that you get them what they need when they need it and that you're generally helpful and make their jobs easier. They don't remember the specifics about what you presented or how fast they got it. They won't care that you canceled dinner plans to rush a project or worked through your vacation. They just won't. But you will. And the resentment and burnout will build up and consume you if you're not careful.

Going above and beyond can also backfire, especially with new clients (which is when we're most likely to do it). In the short term, cutting costs, providing more, or working faster makes a great impression, but it sets the expectation that that's how you'll always work. Your clients will learn to expect more from you, and you'll find yourself in a mess of your making—either working faster and cheaper to keep those clients happy or dealing with their disappointment on a regular basis.

So do yourself a favor and keep it simple: Give your customers what you say you're going to give them when you say you're going to give it to them. That doesn't mean that it's never worth going out of your way to provide an extra service or go the extra mile (literally!), but it's not necessary—or even a good idea—to do it regularly. Putting your effort into keeping your promises, not exceeding them, is all you need to do to maintain your reputation and keep happy clients.

TAKE THE Next Step

GOOD

☐ Stop doing extra work and just do what you promised you would do.

BETTER

☐ Take a minute to think about what you can realistically provide in any given scenario. Then respond.

BEST

☐ Include some extra time and budget into estimates for new clients. Save the extra services for existing clients who have earned that level of service from you.

Expect to work *hard.*

Working for yourself is just that—work. Even if you love what you're doing and love the people you do it with and the people you do it for, it's still work. And sometimes it sucks. There's always something to do, whether for a client or your own business, and the buck stops with you.

I will admit that there are a few times a year when I'm feeling totally burned out and drained by a difficult client, and I'll allow myself dream about how simple it would be to simply show up at a job in the morning, do whatever work someone tells me to do, and go home at the end of the day with a paycheck in hand, not giving a damn about the office. Sounds so easy and free.

But then I think about having to search for and interview for that job. Having to clock in and out. Asking for time off. Commuting. Weird coworkers. Not having control over the work I'm doing. Being unable to say no to extra work. A set paycheck that doesn't change without a fight.

After twenty years of being on my own, I still think that the worst day of being my own boss is a million times better than being bossed around by someone else—even a good boss. No one else will ever give me the flexibility or the money I can choose for myself, so it's worth every bit of hustle, sweat, and sometimes even tears.

What happens when you're not in the mood to work?

We've all had days where we're tired or feeling lazy or just don't feel like working. When you worked for someone else, chances are you got dressed and went to work anyway—docked pay and angry bosses are pretty powerful motivators. When you're on your own, the consequences of slacking off aren't usually as obvious, so it can be tempting to procrastinate and give in to the desire to do nothing. But unless you're independently wealthy, you need to push past the feelings and get to work—your mood doesn't matter.

That doesn't mean there's *nothing* you can do when you're feeling stuck. When lack of motivation hits me, which it does, I look at my to-do list, pick one thing to focus on, and get that done. Or if the items on my list are larger, I pick one and work on it for fifteen minutes. Just doing something is often the push I need to keep going.

The Pomodoro Technique is a way of looking at time in twenty-five minute chunks. Lindsay is a copywriter who uses it daily. "One thing that helps me get going when I'm not feeling it is the free little Pomodoro extension I have on my browser. When my brain is feeling overwhelmed at the thought of work, I'll tell myself, 'I'm going to work for only one Pomodoro. Whatever amount of work I get done during that time—great! But just one Pomodoro, at least, and once that's done, we'll see how I feel.' I'll set the timer, turn on a website-blocking app like LeechBlock (also a free extension), and get to work. Inevitably, the timer will end, I'll hit a groove and will do a few more blocks."

Veronica is a virtual assistant who likes to move around when she needs a mood booster. "I'm able to work in different locations of my home, and the change of scenery seems to help. I can't always afford to go to a coffee shop or access to a coworking space, but God bless libraries! A place to sit and work for free that's decently quiet, set up for study (and work), and free Wi-Fi. I'll go to the library and work for a few hours, allowing myself to browse the books in my downtime." Other people prefer to get away from the computer and go for a walk, organize their space, do some housework, or take a long lunch.

For me, deadlines are very powerful motivators—I don't miss them. When I'm really busy, it's easy to get in the work groove and keep going, even if I'm not loving what I'm working on that day. But when work slows down or when I'm delegating a lot of my to-dos to other people, I really struggle to get going. So if something on my schedule doesn't have a hard deadline and I'm having trouble getting to work on it, I email the client to let them know when they'll get it from me—usually the next day. That way I have to get it done regardless of how I feel and can't keep pushing it off.

What to do on the days where it really sucks?

Pretend it doesn't, at least to clients. You don't have to be fake and say that everything is sunshine and roses, but clients don't want to know that you don't feel like working today. If there's something on your plate that you don't want to do, figure out how you can offload it or get the support you need to just get it done and move on. If you need advice with a tricky situation, find someone to talk to who's likely been there before. If you're really struggling with an emotional issue—we'll talk more about this later in the book—find a therapist, take time off, or find something else that will help you get through for the moment, like ice cream.

Remember why you're working for yourself. Make a list of all of the things you used to hate about your job (see the paragraph above) and then make a list of all of the awesome things you get to experience now. My list looks like this.

- I don't have to drive to work.
- I don't have to shower in the morning or put on nice clothes.
- I can work from anywhere—even the beach (but it's too sandy).
- I can choose whether to work with any client on any project.
- I can work whenever works best for me.

- I don't have annoying coworkers.
- I don't have to ask permission to make an appointment or run an errand or even play hooky.
- I can listen to whatever I want as loud as I want.
- I can do laundry and bake a cake while I'm working.
- I can volunteer at my son's school when I feel like it.
- I can make as much money as I want.
- If something isn't working for me, I can adjust my business and fix it.

When I start dreaming about a "simpler" life working for someone else, I think about this list. It doesn't always make me feel better in the moment, but it helps me keep going.

What to do if it really *really* sucks for a long time?

If you're finding that you're having bad days more often, then it's a good time to rethink what you're doing. Are there particular types of projects or clients that are making you miserable? Can you stop doing those in the future? Do you need to rethink your work-life balance or how you're structuring your day? Do you need to take some little time off or are there small adjustments you can make throughout the day to give yourself some space?

Remember that you're the boss, and you can change your situation at any time. Maybe you can't change it overnight, but you can change it nonetheless. Pivot and go in a different direction. Fire clients. Stop doing certain kinds of work you hate. Start doing more of the work you love. Delegate work to contractors. Find a retainer client for a bit of stability or drop one for a change of pace. Switch up your office or change your scenery, even if that just means taking your laptop into the kitchen for the afternoon. Look into childcare or talk with your partner about getting a better balance at home. Consider collaborating with or bringing on a business partner. Take some time to volunteer or get a part-time job. Or even close up shop and work for someone else full-time. Figure out what isn't working for you and decide what you want to do about it.

TAKE THE
Next Step

GOOD

☐ Make a list of the things that you love about working for yourself and refer to it often.

BETTER

☐ Pick one of the things on your list and lean into it. Spend even a few minutes doing that thing or reveling in it, just because you can.

BETTER

☐ Figure out what motivates you when the going gets tough. Look at what you can change about your situation to have fewer tough days.

Be careful with coaching, classes, and other content.

When you're a newbie, it's normal to feel like you have more questions than answers (I still feel that way sometimes!) and that there's a coach out there who can tell you exactly what to do and make you feel better if you pay them enough. Part of that is true. Someone will always be happy to take your money, whisper sweet nothings into your ear, and tell you what they think you should do, but it's quite possible that they'll just be blowing smoke up your you-know-what. Especially if they're not experienced in the type of business you're running.

In general, don't spend money you don't have on something that isn't absolutely critical. Especially if it means that you're taking away from the ability to actually run your business.

My friend Kristy Lund sells her paintings online, but she was feeling pulled to have her own space where she could showcase her art, partner with other artists, and be around beautiful things in general. We were talking through what she might need to do to start that process, and she mentioned that she was considering signing up for a few sessions with a local business coach. It would be expensive and would really stretch her available budget, but she thought maybe she should do it. I urged her to carefully consider whether it was worth it.

The same holds true for classes, groups, conferences, and seminars. Think critically before spending the money, especially if you're low on funds. Is the class really something you need right now? Do you trust the presenter? Do you reasonably have the money to spend, and if the class turns out to be a bust, how much will you regret the purchase? Is there a way to get that information for free somewhere else or wait and get it later?

I fell into the coaching trap early on. I'd been in business for a few years and felt like I was struggling to find my footing (looking back, I wasn't). I had plenty of work but didn't *feel* successful, whatever that means. At a chamber of commerce networking event, a very nice older gentleman in a fancy suit sensed my doubt and invited me to coffee to talk about my business. I was thrilled to get some advice from someone who had been around a while. An hour later, I found myself handing over a credit card and signing up for a year of monthly coaching for thousands of dollars that I really didn't have to spare. If I'd paid better attention, I would have seen up front that he was a typical sales guy who worked with big corporate clients and was not the right fit for me. Most of his advice had very little to do with what I was trying to do, and to this day I can only remember one piece of guidance that I use. Everything else was a waste of time and money, and frankly, of my self-confidence.

I worked briefly with another coach after him which was better but still not what I really needed—and more money than I should have spent. It wasn't until I found my mentor, Ilise Benun, that I finally got it right. I met her at a graphic design conference (I was in the right place), she only works with creative folks (that's me!), and I didn't have to break the bank or commit a huge chunk of my time upfront. I was able to try her out as I needed help, and we clicked—I've been meeting with her for over ten years, and it's probably the best business decision I've ever made.

To be done well, coaching and mentoring require a good personal connection and lots of trust, so if you feel that you need help, make sure you talk to a few different people and take it slow. If you have colleagues who have mentors, ask for recommendations. Be careful of spending money you don't really have or signing long contracts on something that's largely unknown. With so much information available on the internet, there may very well be a better place to find what you need and still be able to pay your rent.

☑ TAKE THE ☑ Next Step ☑

GOOD

☐ Look for free advice first, whether it's online articles or a conversation with a friend who knows what they're talking about.

BETTER

☐ Sign up for a free or low-cost trial with a coach, class, or service to try it out. Make sure it's really relevant to your situation.

BEST

☐ Find a coach, mentor, or class that's in your industry, relevant to what you really need, and in a price range you can afford.

Don't wait for perfection—just get started.

If you're waiting for everything to be perfect before starting something, whether it's your business or a marketing campaign, you're waiting too long. Perfection is a myth. Nothing will ever be exactly right, and you'll waste precious time and energy trying to make it so.

Especially when you're just starting out or pivoting to something new, it's easy to hesitate when you don't feel like you know all of the answers, and that can lead to paralysis.

Justin Gasparovic, founder of The Enemy of Average, says, "If I could start over today, I would have avoided consuming so much content from business coaches on YouTube, podcasts, and other mediums and put more time into simply doing the work. At a certain point, you have to get out of analysis paralysis and just take action. As you take action and throw yourself in the fire, you'll start to learn the lessons that many of the experts in your niche preach, only you'll have more real-life experience to match that advice. There's nothing wrong with consuming content from people who know more than you, just don't overdo it, and keep in mind that they won't necessarily teach you exactly what you really need to know."

The better path? Get the minimum in place and get started. You don't have to have the entire business plan mapped out in advance—just start looking for clients. You don't have to have a huge portfolio site or a full marketing campaign ready to go—just start putting yourself out there.

My friend Kristy from the last section did this. Instead of shelling out money for a coach, she set up a pop-up shop, Lund Art & Vintage, at a vacant store near her house. Initially, she planned to sell her paintings and vintage clothing for one month, but the shop was so successful that she extended the pop-up for a second month, and then ended up signing a two-year lease. She wouldn't have known what the market was like for a store like hers without trying it out. A coach wouldn't have been able to tell her that—and would have taken her money in the process.

I wish I had started writing my newsletter sooner. I always felt like I had to have a ton of things to say, with a big batch of content written and a full list of ideas on the back burner, before I could send the first email. That wasn't the case at all. I started by writing one. I had a few other ideas in my head for future emails, but I have essentially been winging it ever since. Sometimes I have a topic in mind, and other times I come up with something quick on the fly. Most of the time I'm pleased with what I write and happy to put it out into the world, but there are times when a newsletter needs to get out, and I write something that's good enough. If I waited until those emails were perfect, I'd still be working on them.

Podcaster Gabrielle Ianniello calls this "embracing the f*ck it." She started her podcast as a hobby after quitting a job, and she wasn't prepared when it took off. "I wished I had said 'f*ck it' sooner. I was so caught up in the careful planning and strategizing that often it derailed me from taking action (the most important part) or prevented me from going with the flow as things rapidly changed around me. Like most of us, we're conditioned to think that we need to abide by five-year plans and take rational, methodically-structured action, and yet I've found that to be counterproductive in business. When I learned to abide by my own internal compass and embraced the 'f*ck it' mentality, things started to get *really* exciting. The smartest person doesn't win—the boldest does."

So even if you're not feeling 100 percent ready, get started anyway. You'll learn on the fly, and the learning you do will be more valuable than any learning you get by watching.

Need a quick to-do list?

Here are my top ten things to do next.

1. Create a budget. Include the must-haves (rent, taxes, food), and then any nice-to-haves (vacations, contractor fees, retirement). Know what you *need* to earn, and also what you *want* to earn.
2. Get an EIN number.
3. Sign up for separate checking and savings accounts.
4. Find a good accountant.
5. Start saving, even if it's just a few dollars a month.
6. Narrow down what work you want to do and who you want to do it for, and update your elevator pitch to reflect that.
7. Update (or create) your website and target it to your dream clients.
8. Find a mentor or join groups where you can ask for help from people who are in your field.
9. Find your people. Get to know people who will support you, refer you, partner with you, and serve as your plan B.
10. Market yourself smart. Figure out where your prospects are and promote yourself in whatever way makes sense for you.

TAKE THE Next Step

☑ ☑

GOOD

☐ Clearly define what you want to start in one sentence: "I want to start a
_____." Write down three things you must have in order to start, and do
or get those three things. Forget the rest and start.

BETTER

☐ Now that you've gotten started, make a list of three more things that will
help you improve your process or make it easier to keep going. Do those,
or figure out who can help you get them in place.

BEST

☐ Make a list of what is and isn't working for you at this point. What
can you adjust? Who can help? What else do you need that you don't
already have? Prioritize the items on your lists and work through them
one at a time. Then repeat.

NOTES

Celebrate the little wins—they add up.

Celebrating the big wins, like landing a juicy new contract, is easy. But those wins are likely few and far between. Celebrating the smaller wins and milestones that happen every day might feel a little silly, but I'd argue that those are the more important ones to acknowledge—they're the stepping stones that make the big wins possible.

What sorts of smaller wins might you celebrate?

- Writing a first draft of your next newsletter.
- Getting a submission on your website's contact form that isn't spam.
- Getting a call from a potential new client.
- Completing a big deadline or meeting a milestone on the way to that deadline.
- Figuring out a technical issue.
- Working through a creative block and coming out the other side with an idea.
- Getting a check in your mailbox.
- Getting a testimonial.
- Finally getting an old invoice paid.
- Sending invoices on time.
- Clearing a number of emails in your inbox.
- Starting a task that you don't feel like doing.
- Completing a task that you don't feel like doing.
- Firing a client who no longer fits.
- Finishing your bookkeeping for the month.
- Doing outreach to a group of prospects you really want to work with.
- Getting any response at all (positive or negative) to that outreach.
- Updating your website.
- Sending out a proposal.
- Nailing the presentation you gave this afternoon.
- Showing up at a networking event.
- Focusing on the task at hand and avoiding distractions for an hour.
- Setting a boundary and sticking to it.

How might you celebrate those wins?

- Tell a friend, family member, or colleague who supports you and will get it.
- Share it with an accountability partner.

- Announce it on social media.
- Break out the champagne or sparkling cider or some other treat you don't normally have.
- Treat yourself to something that makes you happy, even if it's small or just takes a few minutes—like a coffee or dinner from your favorite restaurant or ten minutes in your garden.
- For a really big win, treat yourself to something bigger like a trip or a piece of jewelry.
- Simply take a moment to step away, stand tall, breathe deep, and smile.

There are lots of things you can celebrate and feel good about, and they'll be totally personal to you. Recognizing the small things will make you feel good, give you the motivation to keep going, and build confidence. Making progress feels really good, so focus on that rather than on the larger goal at hand. You'll get there eventually.

TAKE THE Next Step

GOOD

☐ Find one small thing to celebrate and acknowledge it.

BETTER

☐ Share a success with someone in your world who will celebrate it with you.

BEST

☐ Acknowledge the small wins and take time to fully rejoice in the big ones—don't let them pass by without some sort of celebration.

YOU ~~don't~~ WANT
TO PERSUADE
~~EVERYONE~~
TO BUY FROM YOU;
YOU WANT THE
RIGHT
PEOPLE
TO BUY FROM YOU.

— MARC WAYSHAK

Most people you encounter are not your customers. They don't need what you offer, don't need you right now, or won't be a good fit for any number of reasons. So stop wasting your time trying to sell to everyone. Instead focus on finding the right people. Let's talk about how to do that.

FIND GOOD CLIENTS

Be picky about clients.

Now that you know who you want to work with, it's time to get to work and try them out. Yep, you read that right—*you're* trying *them* out. *You* get to decide if they are the kind of people you want to work with. Yes, it's a two-way street and they have a say in it, too, but you can't control what clients do, so stay focused on your end of the relationship.

The biggest thing is knowing the choice is yours and developing the insight and guts it takes to stick with what works best for you. Be choosy about who you spend your time with (your mom was right when she told you that in high school). That doesn't mean that you only work with people you like on a personal level—they have to be a fit for you professionally too. If a prospect or client doesn't honor your process, value your expertise and time, or do their part—or if they're not respectful in general—then you can choose not to work with them or work with them again.

If the person you thought was your ideal client isn't, whether because of personality or industry, change it up. It doesn't have to be a major overhaul—maybe you look in a different department or a similar industry.

Once you find those clients—we'll talk more about that later in this section of the book—let them know how much you value them throughout the whole process. We're not talking showering with gifts or praise or letting them walk all over you to make them happy—just take care of them. What are some easy ways to take care of a client?

- Be pleasant. Friendly people are much nicer to work with than grumps.
- Follow through on what you say you'll do. No matter what kind of work you do or who your clients are, they're looking for someone they can trust to help them solve a problem. Be that person.
- Offer suggestions for additional services or products that might benefit them. For example, if you're writing some new case studies for a local manufacturing company, maybe you suggest that they interview some of their users and then share those stories on LinkedIn or social media. And of course, you can help them with that additional offering for a fee.
- As you surf the web or read trade publications, if something reminds you of a client or sounds like it might be interesting to them, send them a note and tell them about it.
- If you're working on a project for another client that they might find interesting or relevant, share it. Maybe the new website plug-in you're using on another site could be helpful to add to theirs. Or maybe the upcoming conference you're attending might be a great marketing opportunity for them.
- Listen and be generous. Maybe you're in a meeting and your client makes an offhand remark that they need to find a new plumber or are trying to find good keto dessert recipes. If you can share a resource, do it! Anything you can share to help make their life easier is a great way to endear people to you. Bonus points if it has nothing to do with something you're trying to sell.
- Make recommendations. If a client needs a service you don't offer, recommend someone you trust. Save the client the time of having to research options.
- Offer to take a task off their hands. Often your expertise will enable you to do a task quickly that feels like a burden to them. One of my clients wanted to create a pocket folder recently and was printing it at a specific online company. I know from experience that all online vendors like their files set up differently, so rather than ask the client to find out the design specifications for me, I told her I'd look them up and set up my files accordingly. She appreciated not having to take the time to do that,

and I appreciated knowing the specs up front and not having to redesign or fix it later.

- Use your network to help support their efforts. Does one of your clients have an upcoming event that other people in your network might be interested in? Share it! If there's a way to showcase some of the work you're doing in support of that effort—like designing the event signage or writing the fundraising emails—it can be a win for both of you.
- Be proactive and try to find solutions or answers before asking them. On a recent conference guide project, the client provided me with a folder of speaker headshots, many of which had clearly been pulled from the web and were small and blurry. I could have asked her to reach out to the speakers and ask for higher-resolution photos, but it generally takes a long time to get people to respond (and most people don't know what makes a photo high-resolution anyway). So I got on the web and tracked down some better-quality versions of most of the images. I let the client know that I had done that when I sent the first draft, and we were able to figure out a plan for the other images.

Ultimately this list is really about listening to your clients and thinking about their needs. Making their work lives easier makes your clients feel valued—and makes them value you. If you focus on benefiting them, they'll come back for as long and as often as they can, creating a mutually beneficial relationship.

TAKE THE *Next Step*

GOOD

☐ Change up your mindset. You are auditioning clients, not the other way around.

BETTER

☐ Look at your list of current clients and prospects. Home in on the ones you love, and find more of those types of people to work with.

BEST

☐ Pivot away from any clients that aren't working for you.

NOTES

Pay attention to red flags.

You can't always know up front whether a prospect will be a good client or not, but there are some common red flags that might signal trouble to come, and you'll learn more as you gain experience and learn what works best for you. The pit in your stomach can be one of your greatest allies—don't ignore it.

What are some red flags you might see?

- Clients who complain about the last person they worked with, especially if the complaints seem unreasonable to you.
- Clients who don't show up for meetings or don't respond to emails and phone calls.
- Clients who pay late or don't pay at all.
- Clients who ask you to rush every project or change the agreed-upon timeline. Extra flags if they then sit on said rush projects after you deliver your part.
- Clients who nickel and dime you or try to talk you into decreasing your rates or doing more for less.
- Clients or prospects who ask for free work. A prospective client should be able to gauge your abilities by talking with you and looking at samples that you provide. If they're asking you to do a test project or do free work to get a job, it's possible that they might steal your ideas and not hire you for the full project anyway.
- Clients who ignore personal boundaries, like texting you at all hours of the night.
- Clients who blame you when stuff goes wrong, even if it's their fault.
- Clients who refuse to sign a contract.
- Clients who don't know what they want, can't articulate what they're looking for, or can't give concrete feedback, and who don't respond in a helpful manner when you try and help them understand and articulate what they need. "Give it more pizzazz" is not feedback you can use.
- Clients who micromanage you while you're working, or who believe they know how long something should take and micromanage your time accordingly.
- Clients who change the scope or project direction in a major way (or even minor ones) every time you work together. Extra flags if they don't agree to the pricing increases that result from those changes.
- Clients who are unorganized, overworked, or unable to delegate.
- Clients who have core values or worldviews that don't mesh with yours. Know your limits in terms of racism, homophobia, or extreme political

views, as well as products and services that make you uncomfortable, like smoking, alcohol, or vaping.
- Clients who are disrespectful or otherwise don't practice common courtesy.
- Clients who don't have funding or who have unreasonable goals, and who won't be swayed to adjust their wants or expectations. You can't guarantee that your mailer design will attract 1,000 new clients or that your fundraising appeal verbiage will increase donations by 50 percent, or that your social media campaign will earn them $5,000 in new sales. Anyone who thinks you can or who wants to pay you according to that expectation shouldn't be your client.

Not all of the items above are necessarily a deal-breaker on their own, but some are. While many of them are general professionalism, some vary based on who you are and your values. Trust your instinct. If you have a gut feeling that signing on with a particular client will bring misery, listen to it. It can be hard to do this when you're just starting out, but as my colleague Alli, a free-lance editor, says, "A bad client, no matter how much they pay, will always take time and energy that could be better spent on fruitful relationships."

Over time you'll know which of these are deal-breakers for you and you can say no early on. If a client develops some of these bad habits over time, use your best judgment to decide whether to change the behavior or end the relationship.

TAKE THE
Next Step

GOOD

☐ When your gut tells you that something is up, pay attention.

BETTER

☐ Write down any flags that you're noticing, and brainstorm some possible solutions that you can share with your client.

BEST

☐ Decide which behaviors are your deal-breakers. Stop working with clients who are badly behaved and aren't willing to change.

NOTES

Show up where your clients are.

Now that you know who your ideal clients are, go get them! But where?

Think about where they hang out. What do they read? Are they active on social media? What groups do they belong to? Here are some places you can start looking.

- LinkedIn.
- Social media—Facebook, X, Instagram, TikTok, Threads, Mastodon, Spoutible, Bluesky, Post ... the list goes on.
- Networking groups.
- Online social groups.
- Trade groups and associations.
- Conferences.
- Trade shows.
- Webinars, classes, and trainings.
- Volunteer organizations.
- Book of lists (compilations of industry lists from local or national business organizations).
- Newspapers or media stories/announcements.
- Magazines or other publications.

Still not sure where they are? Ask an existing or prospective client what groups they belong to or what conferences they're attending. Ask colleagues where they go to look for clients, especially if they're in a similar market.

Once you have an idea of where your target clients are, go there. Join the organization or attend the conference if you can. Get in the room (even if it's virtual) and talk to people. Be curious and ask questions. Participate and be helpful. Get to know the people there and let them see your name. Even if you don't say anything, just show up. If you're in the same places, over time your face and name will become familiar, and people in the group will trust you.

Become a detective. Figure out what your ideal client cares about. What are their biggest challenges? What are they worried about? What are they excited about? What do they love (or hate) about what they do or the industry they're in? What are they reading? Those questions can lead to a gold mine of information that you can use to market yourself. The better you know your ideal client, the better you can help them. Learning is one of your primary goals, especially when you're starting out.

As you get more established, helping is a vital concept. Whatever you do, do *not* show up at the event in sales mode, thinking only about what you can get out of it—the smarmy salesperson is gross, nobody wants that person around, and it won't get you the work. Who do people want to be around? The person who shows up and asks questions, offers relevant information, and can have a nice conversation with no strings attached.

I got one of my favorite clients by attending a nonprofit conference. I sat on a social media roundtable discussion, with no intention of doing anything other than finding out what my ideal clients were thinking about or doing to market themselves. Eight of us had a lovely discussion for an hour, and then went on our merry ways—I didn't even hand out business cards. Six months later, one of the women at that table searched me out via the event attendee list and called me about a project. All she remembered was that I was a designer, that I had information to share, and that I was nice to talk to. That's all it took.

Peer groups are great too! One of the best decisions I've made in the last few years is to join a local "Nonprofit Coffee" group here in Seattle. It's a group of consultants in varying industries who all serve nonprofit clients, and we get together virtually a few times a year to give each other advice, talk about best practices, and have great conversations about the nonprofit world, business ownership, and life in general. Our clients are not in the room and none of us are selling anything—we're all there to learn from each other and have meaningful conversations with like-minded folks. The surprising result? Those connections have resulted in several projects with dream clients that I would never have gotten otherwise. A web designer pulled me in on a big project he was working on, and a copywriter introduced me to her client that needed help on some print projects. A fundraiser hired me to update his own site. And on the flip side, I now have lots of contacts with all sorts of skills that I can refer or call on as my own clients need help. It's a winning situation all around!

I also belong to a few groups of creative folks that work in similar ways. We're not competing with each other, but instead, we're developing deeper relationships that end up fostering partnerships in other ways.

Kieran is an interior designer who does this too. "A big lesson I've learned the hard way is to treat the people in the same industry as you as your friends and network—not everyone is out to compete with you. Starting out, I was always working on my own. I started from scratch and was extremely proud of what I was able to build. However, I was so focused on the competition that I completely forgot about networking with other people in the same industry as mine. There were times when I couldn't keep up with what was happening in the industry and with my peers, and although it feels like it shouldn't matter, it does. It's a good idea to be competitive in business, especially when you're in a market that's saturated. However, you should never avoid opportunities to network and even be friends with your competitors. It is through this that you will be able to grow and learn, and you never know when additional opportunities might arise through these connections."

TAKE THE
Next Step

GOOD

☐ Ask five clients where they typically live online. Look at their websites to see what social media platforms they use and what events they blog about.

BETTER

☐ Join online groups or forums in your industry and participate by commenting on other people's posts and asking questions.

BEST

☐ Find an industry conference or event and sign up. Better yet, be a speaker at the event.
☐ Get published in an industry magazine or on a relevant website.

Market smart, not hard.

Marketing gives you control of your business. Marketing doesn't have to be hard, and selling what you do doesn't have to be icky or uncomfortable.

When I first started my company, marketing generally meant one of these things.

1. **Direct mail.** Purchasing a list, designing and printing a mailer, and sending it out. Which cost time and money that I didn't have.
2. **Networking.** Showing up at a local business event in a room full of people trying desperately to sell stuff. Yuck.
3. **Cold calling.** On the phone. Just writing those words makes me feel sick.

None of those methods appealed to me. I tried them all, barely, and got nowhere. I was fortunate that I had plenty of work to do through repeat clients and referrals. But sticking with whatever clients came my way meant I didn't have much control of my business.

Advances in technology have certainly helped—it's a lot easier and cheaper now to find and reach out to new customers, and to have them find and reach out to you. There are lots of ways to sell yourself, so it's all about finding what fits you, your business, and your ideal clients. Here are some options, but you can also look around your industry or your target clients' industry and see what others are doing.

Write content or hire someone to ghostwrite it for you

Writing content doesn't have to be hard. You have expertise that can help your clients, often even more than you think. I used to think that there was no way I could ever create content for my business, and I marveled at how other writers and marketers always had something to say. I could never do that. But I was wrong! Here are a few ideas to get you started.

- You know a ton about what you do and how you do it, and your customers might have no idea what goes on behind the scenes. So tell them about it. What is your process? Why do you do certain things the way you do them? What does it mean when you use certain terms or lingo? Helping clients to understand the why of things not only gives them a window into what you do but also it can help make the process smoother when you work together.

- Write about questions that your clients ask you. Chances are, if one customer doesn't know what something means, how it works, or why it's needed, there are other people who don't know that either. Remember: just because something makes sense to you or seems obvious, it likely isn't to someone who isn't in your field or doing what you do.
- You know what's important to your customers. What are they worried about? What problems do you solve for your clients, and how do you solve them? What do they need your help with? Write about that. Not only will it showcase your expertise, but other potential clients in the same field will read it and realize that they need your help too.
- You know what can happen when people don't use you or another professional and try to do things for themselves. What pitfalls do they encounter? What time, money, or headaches can they save by hiring a professional? Sell your services without selling your services.
- Tell people a bit about yourself. You don't have to go into great detail about the most personal aspects of your life, but sharing some overall information about who you are as a person and how that relates to what you do helps potential clients connect with you. People like working with people they can relate to and trust.
- Write a case study about a project you worked on, an award you won, or an awesome experience you had with a client.
- Is there a big industry event happening? Or a conference or talk that you attended? Write about what you learned.
- Use AI prompts in ChatGPT or Perplexity to get ideas for content. You'll need to do some digging for the right prompts, but it can be a fun way to come up with some out-of-the-box ideas that might be interesting to your people.

As you write more and more, you'll see potential content everywhere, and you'll be more comfortable writing and sharing your writing. And the writing you do can be really simple. You don't need to have a 1,000-word article or something "important" to say. Something as simple as showcasing your most recent project, announcing an upcoming webinar, or a simple holiday greeting can be a great way to touch base with the folks on your list.

How often do you need to share content? There's no hard rule here, and it depends a bit on where you are in your business and your personal preferences. If you're just starting out or desperate for work, then sharing content as frequently as you can gets you out in front of the most people possible. If you've been around a while and already have a customer base or don't really need new work at this moment, then the frequency is really up to you. Some of my colleagues (writers and coaches in particular) send out emails or post blogs once a week. That's way too often for me—I aim for something monthly-ish. I know people who post something on LinkedIn or TikTok a few times a week, and others who do it every six months. Sending out something—anything—to your existing list reminds them that you exist and that they like you, even if they're not ready to work with you again right now. Do it on a regular-ish basis, even if that's once every quarter, and you'll be top of mind when they are ready and need your help.

Not a writer yourself or short on time? If you have the money and are actually going to do something with the content, then hire someone to write it for you. Copywriters come in at all different price points and are generally really reasonable in my experience. If you are short on funds or are going to let the article they write languish in a folder on your computer somewhere because you don't have the time to do anything with it, then it's not worth the cost. You can also use AI sites to help you get started with bullet points or outlines for an article, but I don't recommend using them to write for you—you'll sound just like everyone else, and the goal here is to have your content sound like *you*. A bot can't really do that, and it'll be obvious to your readers that you didn't write it yourself. So if you go this route, get the inspiration you need, and then say it in your own words.

Once you've got your content ready, post it wherever you can—your monthly newsletter, as an article on LinkedIn, as a blog post on your website, as a guest post on someone else's blog or in relevant industry publications or websites, broken up into smaller social media posts ... the possibilities are endless.

Not sure where to find a writer or other service partner? Ask colleagues or clients who they use. Do a search in your area. Look at LinkedIn. Go to one of your networking groups and ask for referrals. Look for groups online, like Freelancing Females or Millo, and see who is advertising their services there. Post a job on Fiverr or Upwork. Visit trade organization websites like the Graphic Artists Guild or the American Writers and Artists Institute. There are lots of people out there who might be a great fit for what you need, but the only way to find the right fit is to try a few people out and see how it goes.

Email outreach

Email outreach can mean a few different things. It could mean sending a simple note to a past client to say hello and see if they need help. It could mean forwarding an article you read to a potential customer and letting them know that it reminded you of them. It could mean something more like a multi-step email campaign to a new prospect sent over the course of a few weeks. However you do it, know that it works—as long as you're authentic and honest. People can smell bullshit from a mile away, so if you're just looking for a sale with a generic pitch, they'll delete your email immediately.

Want to send an email newsletter as part of your outreach but don't have a list of people to send anything to yet? That's OK! Building a list takes time and a little bit of effort, but it's totally doable. Here's how I built mine—and continue to grow it.

- Start with the people you know who support you. That might include family and friends, former clients and colleagues, vendors you've worked with in the past, or current customers.
- Connect with prospects and colleagues on LinkedIn. Ask if they want to be included on your list to receive occasional emails from you.
- Reach out to members of any groups you're in and ask if they'd like to stay connected via your email newsletter too.
- Attend a conference, class, or webinar, and connect with the people you meet via LinkedIn or an email message. Ask if you can keep in touch with them by adding them to your contact list.
- When you reach out to prospects, or when potential customers reach out to you, ask if you can add them to your list so that you're top of mind when they need help.
- Offer some sort of freebie on your website and collect emails as part of the download process.

Keep in mind that you don't need a huge list—you're looking for quality over quantity. A handful of people who will use your services and recommend you is worth more than a long list of people who don't know you and don't care. And however you build your list, check the email laws in your country or district to make sure you're compliant.

Social media

Posting on social media and connecting with people is a great way to keep in touch and stay visible. Where you post will depend on where your clients tend to be and what you do. LinkedIn is the best place to start, in my opinion—almost everyone who is in a business has some sort of presence there, and it's a great way to find and join groups and get connected to people you want to work with. If you're in a creative field, Instagram or TikTok might be another place to showcase your work. The key with any social media is to be where your clients are and to also pick the platforms that make sense for you personally. If you hate X or Facebook, then don't bother with it. Or hire a social media person to do it for you.

Practice thought leadership

What does that mean? It sounds fancy or scary, but basically, it means that you share what you know with people who need or want to hear it. That might mean speaking at a conference or on a webinar or even just attending the conference or webinar and asking questions and being visible. Host your own webinar or teach a class. Join an organization and look for speaking opportunities. Do a podcast interview. Being visible doesn't just introduce you to your ideal clients—it also helps establish you as someone who is experienced and knows what they're talking about, which then helps draw more people to you.

For people early in their careers, connecting with or following other thought leaders can be a good way to build connections and learn, especially if they're in a relevant industry.

Direct mail

People love getting physical mail, especially if it's personal. A well-designed piece will go a long way to help you stand out in the crowd and reach new prospects. A colleague of mine sends nicely typed personalized letters to prospects and gets great results. Another sends a packet with a poster and some wildflower seeds (relevant to the theme of her business). You might send a catalog or a simple postcard. The people who need your services will hold on to it and reach out. But don't waste your time designing (or paying someone to design) and printing something if you don't have the extra money to spend. You very well might send out a mail piece and sign a new client the next day for a big contract that will pay for your mailing and then some, but more likely than not, you'll send something out and not see tangible financial results for some time. If you're short on funding or don't have the design chops to do it yourself, then consider something simple like a note on nice paper that requires minimal effort and the cost of a stamp.

Volunteer for a relevant organization

Volunteering just to sell something feels dirty, but if you have the right intentions, it can be a great way to let people know who you are. I'm currently the PTA president at my son's school and have served as the vice president in charge of fundraising for the past two years. It's a win for me: I get to help raise money for a cause I believe in (students and education), help figure out how to spend that money in the ways that best support our school, do fun things with my son, meet new friends, and do graphic design for a nonprofit, which is what I'd be doing at work anyway. It's a win for the school: They're getting my skills and expertise for free and having a passionate volunteer at the ready. And the bonus is that everyone knows that I'm the awesome flyer graphic designer lady. I haven't gotten new clients out of it yet, but people know who I am, and eventually, that will pay off in one way or another—even if it's just because I get to put the samples on my website and feel really good about volunteering. With all these marketing ideas, it's about playing the long game, which we'll talk more about later.

Yes, cold calling works too

I know a few business owners who love talking on the phone and have a lot of success reaching out to new clients by calling them. If you're like them, go for it. I'll be in the corner breathing into a paper bag. You could even try robocalling. A web designer in California that I've never met sends me a re-corded voicemail every few weeks, and even though I find the calls annoying and delete them immediately, I remember his name. And it must be working, because he keeps doing it.

The best strategy

What's the right combination for you or the best place to get started? Whatever you decide, the key is to actually do it. Try a few, and if some of them aren't working for you (meaning you don't do them), then stop and try something else. Your strategy will be unique to you and your business, and it will evolve over time.

That's what happened for Emma's event planning business. "In the early stages of my business, I wasn't really keen on advertising and digital marketing; I was of the belief that if it's a good business, then word would get out on its own, so I depended too much on customer referrals. Due to that belief, there was slow growth at the early stages of my launch. However, if I could go back in time with the knowledge I have now, I would invest in advertising and digital marketing: flyers and posters, email marketing, content marketing, and online advertising. One other thing I would do differently would be to seek partnerships with companies that produce similar and complimentary services to those offered by my company. I recently partnered with a graphic designer and a furniture staging company and the results have been mind-blowing; so it's definitely something I will keep doing."

TAKE THE Next Step

GOOD

☐ Pick one method of marketing that appeals to you, try it a few times, and evaluate how it works for you.

BETTER

☐ Figure out what your minimum maintenance marketing level is and do that. It's the one or two most basic things that you will make time for, as often as you can do it. That might be anything from writing one blog post or sending one newsletter a month, to posting on LinkedIn once a week, to doing outreach once a quarter.

BEST

☐ Choose two or three marketing methods that you like and that you have time for, and do them every week.

Be thoughtful about RFPs.

I think RFPs (request for proposals) are the worst. They're a giant tease, a shiny brass ring just out of reach. In my experience, they're a total waste of time and hope.

A request for proposal is a document that outlines a new project and invites service providers to submit a proposal to do the work. The RFP generally includes the overall project scope, anticipated contract terms, vendor requirements, deliverables, deadlines, and evaluation criteria. They're generally created by larger organizations that need to get multiple bids on any given project—most of the ones I see are from government organizations. RFPs are usually posted online for the public at large; occasionally they might be sent directly to specific vendors that have a relationship with the organization.

In my younger days, I loved them, mostly for the reasons stated above. RFPs are generally put out for really big, shiny projects with bigger clients. The thought of winning the job is really appealing, but it's usually just that—a daydream. In reality, you'll spend a lot of time putting together the perfect proposal that answers every question and shows off your fabulous talent, only to lose the job to the firm the organization was planning on hiring anyway. But the allure is strong enough that a lot of us keep responding to them, at least for a while.

Whether you choose to respond to an RFP depends on a few factors.

- **Consider the source.** If someone in the organization personally invited you to submit a bid, then it's probably a no-brainer that you'll respond, especially if they're one of the decision-makers. If you found it at random doing a web search, then you should think a lot more critically about whether to bother.
- **Consider the project.** Is the project something you have a lot of experience doing, or is it a totally new type of work for you? What sort of examples do you have to show? Would you need to involve other contractors or vendors, or is it something you can do yourself? Assume that other applicants will have a lot of experience with whatever the project is, and consider whether your skills realistically match up.
- **Consider the competition.** Can you find out how many other firms are vying for the same RFP? Are they larger firms or smaller businesses like yours? If you're one of five firms competing, you have a much better shot than if you're one of one hundred.
- **Consider the reason for the RFP.** Companies are often required to get multiple bids for large projects, particularly if grant money is involved.

Does the client have someone in mind that they already want to work with and just need alternative bids for comparison? Or is this a serious RFP that is genuinely open to the best applicant?

- **Consider the reasonableness of the RFP.** What is the proposal process like? How involved is the process, and how much work will it take for you to fulfill the requirements? Do they give enough time to reasonably pull something together, or is the process rushed? Are the directions and requirements clear? Do you have the ability to ask questions and get clarification? What is the review process like? How will the decision be made, and what factors will weigh more heavily than others? If the RFP itself is a mess or vague, then the project likely will be too.
- **Consider the budget.** Is there a budget stated in the RFP? How reasonable is it? If there isn't a budget, how can you find out what it is so that you're at least in the right ballpark?
- **Consider your odds.** Can you get someone from the review team on a call to answer questions in person and talk through the request? Can you walk one of the decision-makers through your proposal when you submit it to answer any questions in real time and get a reaction? Any personal connection you can make increases your odds in general, and you can likely get answers to some of the questions above. At a minimum, see if you can get a direct email conversation with them to answer your questions.
- **Consider your time.** How much time will you need to pull together a proposal like this? Are you starting from scratch, or do you already have a template that you can update? What else do you have on your plate? Rather than chasing after a random project that you might not win, are there other ways you can network or market yourself that are more likely to pay off?

Do some homework, and then you can gauge how likely you are to win the project or waste your time.

TAKE THE
Next Step

GOOD

☐ The next time you find or receive an RFP, weigh the pros and cons. Make note of any red flags.

BETTER

☐ Ask questions, even if it's only via email. Get as much clarity as you can to decide if it's something you want to pursue.

BEST

☐ If you want to pursue it, get someone from the review team on the phone. See if there's a way you can walk the decision-makers through your proposal.

NOTES

Get used to ghosting.

Ghosting isn't just for dating. In fact, with so many more communication channels at our fingertips, the more likely you are to be ghosted—there are so many more places where someone can and will ignore you!

We all ignore random emails, messages, and phone calls that we get from strangers, so here I'm largely talking about people that you're in contact with in some way who then disappear or don't follow through. I've been ghosted by just about every type of person I can think of. I've been ghosted by vendors, contractors (not great), a bookkeeper (*really* not great), clients, and prospects. It happens all the time, so be prepared for it to happen to you, because at some point it will.

The good news is that most of the time the ghosting has nothing to do with you—it's all about the other person. Here are some of the reasons this might happen.

- **Family emergencies.** A prospect and I had been in talks for months and had just agreed on the scope of a really large project. I sent the estimate and ... heard nothing. Turns out her mother had been diagnosed with cancer two days after I sent the estimate. She went on leave, and the project was no longer a priority.
- **A company sale.** Another prospect signed a contract, so I sent over the invoice for the deposit and emailed her to schedule our kickoff call. I got crickets in return. Found out later that the company was sold shortly after the contract signing, and the project disappeared.
- **A new job.** I've had clients quit their jobs, get fired, or go on leave without any sort of notice to me, so whatever we were working on or planning to work on abruptly disappeared.
- **Cold feet.** Sometimes people have second thoughts, especially if it's their own money versus the company's money. I've been ghosted several times because people just couldn't decide to move forward.
- **User error or technology issues.** I've been ghosted by people who later told me that "the email was in my outbox and I forgot to send it" or that they sent it to the wrong email address.
- **Fear.** I've sent more than one proposal over the years and gotten no response because they went with another vendor and didn't want to hurt my feelings.
- **Timing or not a good fit.** My mailbox is full of emails from sales people that I will never respond to, and prospects ignore my outreach every day. Clearly the timing is off or the fit isn't right—we don't need that service right now or at all.

- **Death.** One of my small business clients died suddenly, and I found out about it months later from a mutual acquaintance.

With the exception of someone dying, there's really no way to know if the reasons given are true. In some cases, I know I'm being lied to, but in general, I just have to assume that people have good intentions. In all honesty, their intentions don't make much difference—if you can't get in touch with them, you can't. The only thing you can control is your response.

What can you do about it? Not a lot. Treat every project as a maybe until the money is in your bank account. If the ghost is someone you're already working with or in talks to work with, then it's worth reaching out a few times by email and phone to see what's up. If you are also working with one of their colleagues, you might try reaching out to them to see if they have any answers. If you have an email newsletter, add that person to your list so that you're occasionally coming up in their inbox as a reminder that you exist. If you're still not getting a response, chalk it up to a learning experience and move on.

GOOD

☐ If you think you're being ghosted, don't take it personally.

BETTER

☐ Occasionally reach out to prospects or clients who seem like they might be ghosting you, just in case they're not.

BEST

☐ After a few targeted nudges, move the ghosts to your back burner and move on. Keep them on your general marketing list, but don't make special effort to reach them.

Watch for client expiration dates.

OK, an expiration date sounds a little morbid. Maybe graduation date is a better term, though some departures are less honorable and accomplished. The fact is every relationship in your business will end at some point. There are lots of reasons that people might move on.

- As you grow, you'll want to charge more, and your starter clients might not be up for that.
- You might decide that you want to move into a different niche or do a different kind of work, and some existing clients might not fit within that.
- Maybe you've been working with a client for so long that you're bored with the work and want something new. Or maybe they feel like they need a fresh perspective.
- You might be ready for new opportunities and bigger or different fish.
- A client might grow and decide to bring the work in-house.
- A client might scale back and not have work for you or might want to pay you less.
- Your client may go out of business.
- Your contact might leave the job, and the new person has their own vendors they want to use.
- Maybe that new client that looked really promising just isn't clicking with you, and it's time to move on.

Any of these same things can and will happen with vendors, contractors, or employees who work with you. At some point, what was working won't be cutting it any more, and you'll move on to something or someone else. Sometimes the break is expected and cordial; sometimes it's abrupt and an unpleasant surprise. I find that most of the time, there's a gradual fading away over time—you work together less and less, and there's no real formal ending or hurt feelings.

What happens when a client ends your relationship unexpectedly? Stay calm. If you can, find out why they're making the change, and then you can decide if it's something you can potentially fight for or if it's better to accept it and move on. It's OK to express your disappointment but be gracious—just because they're ending things now doesn't mean they won't be back. Maybe the new vendor they're hiring won't work out. Maybe your contact will leave that job and call you when they get to their next position. Maybe they'll refer you to their colleagues even if they aren't using you. You never know, so leave things on a good note—assuming they've paid you and you want to work with them again.

Once I drove a fancy box of chocolate to a retainer client's office the week before Christmas to wish him a merry Christmas and to say thank you for being such a great client. He told me how much he enjoyed working with me and that he'd be in touch after the New Year. Sure enough, he did get in touch with me on January 2 to tell me that they were ending my contract and moving on with a larger design firm. I was livid that I'd wasted my time and effort on the gift and angry that he hadn't had the courage to tell me the news to my face. There wasn't really much I could do about it, so I swallowed my anger, told him I'd miss working with him, appreciated our work together, and that was that. Over time he referred me to a few other clients, which he wouldn't have done had I told him what I really thought in the moment.

On the flip side, I've ended client relationships too. When I first started out, I lucked into a retainer agreement with a larger design firm, and we ended up working together for years. As their company grew, they brought on additional employees, moved me to an hourly rate, and started giving me less to do every month. At the same time, I was growing my own business and felt like it might be time for us to part ways to create space for other clients. My maternity leave provided the perfect opportunity to end things on an amicable note. Even though it's been over ten years since then, I still occasionally get referrals from them for work that they're too big to do.

If you're working with someone and it's time for them to graduate, just be up front about what's happening and figure out what the ending looks like for you. Do files need to be handed over or final checks cut or referrals made to replacements? Is there a list of tasks that will need to be done after you're gone or after this milestone is complete? You don't need to go into specific detail about why things are coming to a close unless you want to. I've found that keeping it simple is best.

- "I don't think we're a good fit."
- "I'm not doing x type of projects anymore."
- "I'm taking my business in a different direction."
- My schedule is full, and I can't take on your next project."
- Or, ideally, "We've been working together for fifty years, and I'm retiring and moving to Aruba."

All those responses are professional and clean. Even if you would never, ever, ever work for that person or company again, don't burn the bridge. It's generally best to part ways with a client in between projects (or project stages) and with as much advance notice as you can. Unfinished work or rude responses can reflect poorly on you; word gets around, and you never know who else might be watching who may need your services down the line. Handle the situation with professionalism and calm, and save the ranting for family and friends.

Melanie Deardorff, owner of Melanie Deardorff Marketing + Communications, has parted ways with two clients in her career. "In hindsight, I should have acted sooner. The anxiety I felt when they emailed me or when we met on Zoom was a sign. While I don't recall my exact words, I intentionally avoided sharing why they drove me nuts. Instead, I softened the blow, saying something like, 'It's not you, it's me. I can't meet your expectations.' In both situations, I felt an immediate sense of lightness, realizing I wouldn't have to work with them any longer! Sometimes, clients aren't a good fit—and that's perfectly fine."

TAKE THE Next Step

GOOD

☐ Look at your current client list and make a note of any relationships that seem to be winding down.

BETTER

☐ Have some scripts on hand, whether for clients who are graduating themselves, or who you are letting go.

BEST

☐ Pack up all files for any graduating clients and make sure they have what they need to continue on elsewhere.

Play the long game.

Growing your business takes time and regular, sustained effort. If you're sending out a newsletter once a year or posting occasionally on social media and expecting to have new clients beating down your door, you're deluding yourself.

Marketing and growing your business is all about playing the long game. However you decide to put yourself and your business out there, assume that every email you send and every post you write is one more in a long line of steps that will eventually pay off. Chances are, you're not going viral. And even if you do, most of the people who reach out to you aren't clients, at least right now.

I started my newsletter in November 2019. I've sent it out almost every single month since then, and I've gotten a grand total of *one* project directly related to my outreach. And that was from someone I worked with a really long time ago. I also do email outreach, sending campaigns to fifteen to twenty targeted prospects every quarter. Out of those emails, about a third of the people respond at all, and maybe one or two of those is a prospect who I can put on my newsletter list in the hope of getting future work.

So if the payoff is low, and it takes so long to see, why do it?

If you don't put yourself and your business out into the world, it'll be a lot harder for people to find you, if they ever do. You'll also have less control over the narrative and less control over what kinds of customers and clients are available to you.

Getting your message out gives potential clients a window into who you are and what you do and gets your message front and center. They might not be ready to work with you right now, but they might know other people who do need you. When they are ready, you'll be top of mind because they're seeing you in their inboxes and social media feeds. When they reach out to you, they'll already feel like they know you and like you, and they are more likely to be the right fit for you. Prospects who aren't a good fit will self-select out and go elsewhere.

So even if your efforts are small, get out there. The sooner you start, the sooner you'll get a result.

TAKE THE
Next Step

GOOD

☐ Using a preferred method, reach out to your network at least once a quarter.

BETTER

☐ Using a preferred method, reach out to your network at least once a month. Plan it out on a regular schedule.

BEST

☐ Use a calendar or scheduling software to plan out your marketing for the next three months. Automate it.

NOTES

CHARGE WHAT YOU'RE WORTH.

— THOUGHT LEADERS EVERYWHERE

NO!

Your pricing shouldn't be based on what you think you're worth or what you think you can get away with charging. There are real limits to what the market and industry you're in will bear and the value of the service you're providing. That has nothing to do with your personal worth and everything to do with the actual costs to create the project, your experience, and what you need to earn in order to keep the lights on.

MAKE GOOD MONEY

Decide what you charge.

First things first: If you haven't already done so, figure out what you're going to charge, whether that's your hourly rate or a project fee. That will of course vary depending on your location, profession, experience level, and a host of other things. If you already have a rate you've been using, think about how well it's working to meet your goals. And be prepared to raise your rates—often you can charge more than you think.

Determining your rates

How do you figure out what a reasonable hourly rate is in the first place? Look at what people similar to you are charging. Talk to colleagues and see what their rates are or talk to people in your networking groups to find out what they've paid for services similar to yours. I had a friend years ago who worked at a print shop, and he would routinely call his competitors, pretending to be a client with a project, to see what they would charge. Another colleague looks at freelance job boards to see what other writers are charging for certain types of projects and what other potential clients are willing to pay for services like his.

Organizations like the AIGA put out annual salary lists for creative professions, and the Graphic Artists Guild has a fabulous guide for creatives. Look for groups in your industry that do something similar to you to help you know if what you're charging is in the right ballpark.

Keep in mind that no two situations are alike, and no two projects are the same. Use the information you get to influence your decisions rather than dictate them. There will be some trial and error as you figure out what the market will bear, and you may need to make some adjustments to either beef up what you offer for a given price or lower the price and do more of that type of work. Every estimate and every project is a bit of an experiment.

Most importantly, you need to figure out what you need to make to survive. Work up a budget with all of your business and personal expenses, including taxes. Then figure out what that breaks down to hourly based on how much you want to work in a week. If you only have a capacity of twenty hours a week for billable work, you'll likely need to charge more than if you have thirty hours available. Another thing to keep in mind: Even if you're working a full forty-hour week, you won't spend all of that time doing billable work. Assume that five to ten hours each week is spent working on your business (marketing, paperwork, finances, etc.) and budget accordingly.

Don't forget about your own personal goals. If you want to be able to take a three-week vacation to Hawaii every year (yes, please!) or buy a boat, factor that in. Vacations aren't paid when you're on your own, so you'll need to factor in a bit extra in that hourly rate to cover your time off or find an extra project each year to cover it. Any time I want to buy something bigger that I haven't planned for, I try to find another project or two that will cover that cost. Sometimes that works, sometimes it doesn't.

What if a client comes to you and has a particular rate that they want to pay? Assuming it's lower than what you want to charge, and assuming that you want to try and make it work with them, then you'll either need to negotiate a rate that works for both of you or negotiate an overall project fee that you can live with. If that doesn't work, then you'll need to make the decision whether to work with them. The answer to that might be different depending on the type of work it is and how busy you are.

Increasing your rates

When I first went out on my own, I randomly chose $40 an hour as my starting point. That was a little more than double my hourly rate as a salaried worker, so it seemed like that should be plenty of money—no budgeting or math needed. That worked for a little while, but then I wanted to get out of my parents' house and get my own place, so I increased it to $60, still without any real plan or reasoning behind it. The number just sounded good, and I was busy enough that the quantity made up for my low rate.

I repeatedly had clients tell me that I wasn't charging enough for what I was offering (not that they were complaining!), but I didn't consider that I could raise my rate significantly until I got a call from a woman I had met in a networking group. Her mother owned a real estate company and was firing her graphic designer in the middle of a simple brochure redesign. She said, "I'm telling my mom to call you, and you need to charge her $100 an hour for ten hours to get the job." I was stunned—in my limited experience, that was an ungodly sum to pay for a trifold brochure (how times have changed!). But I did as she said and happily cashed that check. It changed everything. That doesn't mean that I jumped to $100 across the board overnight, but it didn't take me long to get there once I knew that it was possible.

You might be thinking, "How do I almost double my rate overnight and not have clients running for the hills or getting angry with me?"

Start by using the new rate with new clients. They haven't worked with you before and don't know any different. It's a great way to test out whether your new rate is too high or not high enough. Winning every project you bid on? Raise the rate or project fee. Losing them all? Assuming there's not another non-monetary reason you're losing out, consider bringing them back down a bit. Or better yet, bid on projects with larger clients who have more money to spend.

Increase rates for existing clients slowly and with advance warning. I hadn't raised my rates in a decade (which I don't recommend), so last October I emailed all of my current regular hourly clients to tell them that I was raising my rates by 10 percent starting January 1. Here's what I said: "After ten years, the time has come for me to raise my rates. Starting January 1, my new rate will be $XXX. I hope that works with your budget and value your business." I will admit that I was really nervous to send that email. Would they all fire me in December? Nope. Thanks to inflation and really good working relationships, the overall response was either "Sure, whatever" or "All of our vendors are doing that, so we expected it." Only one client balked a bit, telling me that I was already too expensive on some projects, but she'd continue to pay it. Had anyone not wanted to continue on, they would have had three months to find a new designer.

What if a current client is paying a really low rate, and bumping them up to your new rate would be a really big jump? You have a few options. If you don't care whether you continue working with them, then you can give them advance notice and just tell them what the new rate is, and they'll decide what to do about that. If you do care about keeping them on, you can either increase the rate a bit each year until they're on par with your new clients, or ideally you can have a conversation about it with them and figure out a compromise that works for both of you. Say, "You and I have been working together for a long time at $XXX per hour, and my newer clients are paying $XXX per hour. I'd like to bring you a bit closer to my new rate. What feels comfortable for you? What about $XXX?" You might not get your full rate with that conversation, but maybe you get closer to it than an incremental increase. And your client will appreciate being a part of the conversation.

What if a new client comes to you and says, "Sonja referred me to you for this same type of project, and she only paid $XXX. Why are you charging me $XXXX?" Ideally, your clients won't share rates when they refer you, but it does happen. All you need to say is that your rates have increased since you started working with Sonja, and she's still grandfathered in at the lower rate. You can also mention that new clients require extra time and attention as you get to know them, and every project is different, so that can absolutely justify a higher project price.

Be wary of people who balk at the price right out of the gate. If you've confirmed the scope and articulated the value that you bring to the table and they're still pushing back, then they're not the right fit for you. A recent trick I learned from a colleague is to be brutally honest about pricing transparency from the start. He was talking to a prospect about a big branding project and when they asked about his rate, he said, "I don't want to scare you off by giving you a big number right now, so let's talk through what you need, and if you're transparent about your budget, I'll be realistic with my numbers, and we can see where we land. Does that work?" That approach might not work for everyone, but I love the way it sets up the relationship on an honest footing.

TAKE THE *Next Step*

GOOD

- ☐ Research businesses similar to yours and see what they are charging.
- ☐ Decide what you want your new hourly rate to be. Say it out loud.
- ☐ Think about a type of project you do a lot of, and increase the price of it in your head by at least 10 percent.

BETTER

- ☐ When your next new client or prospect comes, quote them your higher rate. Test it out.
- ☐ The next time an annual project comes around for an existing client, increase the estimate by 5-10 percent.

BEST

- ☐ Tell your existing clients that your rates/fees are increasing, and give them a month or two advance notice.

Weigh the costs: hourly rate versus project fees.

Ask any two creatives whether they charge by the hour or by the project and you'll get two different answers. There are good arguments to be made on either side, so how you charge for your work is really up to you. There are pros and cons to each, and if you're like me, a mix of the two options might work best.

The case for charging by the project

Charging by the project generally makes things easier—you know how much time you can budget and what you can bill for it, and the client knows what they'll be paying. No surprises. It also allows you to charge more. When you're giving a project quote, you can take into consideration the size of the client (corporations have more money than small businesses) and the overall value of the project to them (what will the client make as a result of your work). It's a lot easier to say that a project will cost $X,XXX to complete than to explain how many hours something will take you and why, and a project rate allows you to increase the fee if it's a genuinely valuable project. Most clients seemingly only care about the bottom line anyway. A client who will make a million dollars as a result of your work should pay more for it, regardless of how long it actually takes to complete.

Another benefit to charging by the project is that the more you do something over time, you'll get better at it. Which usually means you'll get faster at it. Or you'll at least do it with fewer mistakes or a lot more know-how. If you're working hourly, the less time you work and the less money you make (unless you raise your rates exponentially, but still). Your experience should make you more valuable—not less profitable.

You also might be leaving money on the table if you go with an hourly rate. On a recent book project, I asked the client if they had a budget in mind, and they did. They had a grant amount that needed to be spent, and the figure was a lot higher than I would have charged had I gone hourly.

A potential downside to project fees? Estimating. Figuring out how long it'll take you to complete a project can be difficult, especially if it's a new type of work that you haven't done before or the deliverables are vague or unclear. When I'm giving a project quote, I start by figuring out how long I think it will take me (or a contractor) to do the work, and then I include some extra buffer in case I'm underestimating the time. If I do end up underestimating how long something will take, then I have two options: take the loss on the project and learn my lesson or talk to the client and ask for more money (see more on that below).

This happens to Evelyn Ott, a tattoo artist at Soul Canvas Ink, all the time. "I charge based on the size, hours, and the complexity of the flash. Some are quite difficult to achieve, while others come really easily. Sometimes I can determine this by looking at the client's sample, but sometimes I only realize how difficult or simple it is when in the middle of the session. I can't always nail the right price based on a sample—sometimes it's more of a task than I thought. It's very hard to tell a client you underestimated the price because you didn't know how much of a job the tattoo would be. Some agree to give you a bit more, but others stick to the initial price, and I have to just let it go. It's really difficult. It takes real mastery to look at a piece of art and know just how much effort it will take to draw on skin."

The case for charging by the hour

Hourly fees can be great if the project is small or vague. I do a lot of work with shopping malls, and most of the projects are small and have a quick turnaround. In any given month I might do five projects for a single shopping center, and each of those projects has smaller subtasks that need to be done. With thirty chopping centers on my roster, that can add up to a lot of small projects each month. If I had to estimate each of those in advance, I'd spend more time doing paperwork than I would actually doing the job. So going hourly with those particular clients works really well. Most of the projects are similar in scope, so the client knows roughly what to expect in terms of cost, and we have a good level of trust. Over time, I've gotten much faster at completing some of those, so I charge the same amount over time to align with client expectations, and I make more money.

Pricing hourly might also work well in situations where a project has changed in scope. When I'm estimating a project, I include a set number of design rounds, along with a note that any revisions above and beyond those will be billed hourly at $XXX rate. The client is incentivized to keep the project within scope, and I can charge extra if needed.

Another option for hourly pricing that I've encountered lately is to switch to hourly pricing when a project stalls. This works particularly well on a larger, longer-term project like a website. One of my colleagues frequently had web projects stall because clients weren't ready with content or were taking months to make decisions and provide feedback, all of which delayed project payments and derailed project schedules. Her solution? Set milestone payment dates for project fees, with the final payment due on a specific calendar date. If the project stalls, the payment is still due on the originally targeted date, and the project moves to an hourly-fee basis when the client is ready. I haven't tried this myself yet, but I know of several other people who have and are loving the results.

On the flip side, working hourly can be a problem if you take longer than your client is expecting. Sticker shock on an invoice from you is *not* what you want. What to do about that? It depends on the situation. First, figure out why the project is taking longer than you thought.

1. Did you get started without having all of the information you needed?
2. Are you having writer's block or whatever the equivalent creative paralysis is for your work?
3. Did the project scope change?
4. Did you or one of the people on your team have a family emergency or get sick or fry a computer with a coffee spill?
5. Did your planned method of execution not work as expected? Are you having technical or design issues?
6. Did you simply underestimate how long it was going to take to do that particular task?

Be honest and talk with the client about it as soon as you know there's a problem (or even if you suspect there might be one). Explain the issue and figure out what your ask is. Do you need more time? Do you need more money? Are you just giving them a heads up? If you're all on the same page, you can decide together what the best course of action will be. If you're sick and the client can't afford to wait, then maybe someone else finishes the project. If you underestimated the time needed, maybe they'll be willing to at least split the cost difference with you (ideally they'll pay for all of it). You may need to eat the cost and take the loss, especially if the estimating or cost error is yours or if it will save or mend a client relationship. Regardless of the outcome, and even if they aren't thrilled to hear what you have to say, clients will appreciate that you spoke up and aren't just springing the unexpected on them.

What about retainers?

Depending on the setup, retainer agreements can be a win-win for both you and your clients. The basic premise is that you will be paid for a certain number of hours each month, usually at a slightly lower rate. I've had retainers with several of my clients over the years, and I use them with some of the contractors that work for me too. There's a lot of upside for everyone involved—the client can rest easy knowing that they have your time reserved for their work each month and what they'll be paying for it, and you can feel good about having set income coming in each month.

But retainers can have some downsides too, depending on how they're structured. Here are a few things to consider.

- How long will the agreement last? Do you have an ending or re-up date where you can make changes, or will you just make changes on the fly as you or the client need to adjust?
- What happens if you go over the allotted hours in a month? Do the extra hours roll over to the following month, or do you invoice those at your usual rate? (I typically do the latter.)
- What happens if you have unused time at the end of each month? Do you get paid for that time anyway, do you have to make those up in the following month, or do you have to pay the client a refund the unused time at the end of the year? (I once turned down a really nice retainer for that last reason—there's a reason I became a designer instead of an accountant.)
- Will you be expected to put the retainer client first and prioritize their work over other clients regardless of what's on your plate? Can you say no to a retainer project if you're already booked?
- Can you use a subcontractor to help with the work, or does the work have to be done by you because of an NDA or other legal requirement?
- Does a retainer make sense for this particular client? Is the amount of work you do for them pretty steady each month, or are there lots of ups and downs in workload?

Thinking through these questions can help you negotiate the agreement that works best for you. In the right scenarios, retainers can be a fantastic way to get steady work.

Always track your time

It should go without saying that if you're working on an hourly basis, you'll need to track your time. I have a colleague who wings it every month and takes a guess at how long she spent doing certain projects, but I don't recommend that. It feels unethical to charge clients for more time than you spent, and conversely you might be guessing wrong and underestimating how long you spend on something.

But even if you are working on a project basis and no one else will ever know how much time you spent on it, track your time. Be as religious as you can about it, within reason. Knowing how long a given project will take you gives you the ability to estimate more accurately and give ballpark ranges to clients that make sense. It makes estimating much faster and easier, and you'll be less likely to lose money.

What time tracker should you use? There are lots of options—everything from an online paid service (I use Harvest) to using a timer and an excel spreadsheet. The right one is whatever one you'll actually use.

TAKE THE *Next Step*

GOOD

☐ Make a list of your current clients/projects and see if there are any that might benefit from a change to hourly or project billing.

BETTER

☐ When a new prospect comes in, ask them if they prefer hourly or project pricing. If you estimate by the project, add in an hourly rate for any work above and beyond your agreement.

BEST

☐ Losing money on a current project? Figure out why and decide on a fix that works best for you. Can you get more money or cut services, or do you need to eat the cost and learn a lesson from it? Make a note for the next time this type of project comes in and estimate accordingly.

Own your price.

Now that you know your fee and what will work for you personally, don't apologize for it. It's nobody's business why you charge what you charge, and you don't have to explain yourself. Focus instead on your value and what the customer gets by working with you.

When I give a client an estimate, I tell them what it's going to cost, and what the scope entails—how many designs, how many rounds of revisions, any additional services included, and what the final deliverables are. I talk about some of the intangibles that go along with the project—the customer service they'll get, the fact that I've been doing this a long time and know how to solve problems, the fact that I know them or their market and am a trusted resource. I don't explain the internals of why I'm charging what I'm charging, and I don't think most clients care about that. They care about what's in it for them, what they actually get, and the value they place on that.

There will always be someone who thinks you're too expensive or can't afford you no matter what you're charging. When it comes down to it, if they can't or won't pay a price that works for you, it's not a good fit, and work that isn't a good fit can be worse than no work at all.

Don't reduce your prices without a reason

Once you've figured out what you need to charge for a specific project or service, stick to that unless you take something away. When I was starting out, if a client balked at an estimate, I would often reduce the price "to be nice." *Never ever ever* do that. Being nice has nothing to do with running a business. Being nice is a horrible reason to take money off the table and out of your pocket.

If you do decide to reduce a price on something, take something away. Reduce the number of initial designs or rounds of revisions. Reduce the overall scope and take part of the project off. Make sure there's a real, solid reason you're bringing the price down. Even better—create smaller packages. So instead of charging less for the same work, create a new package that has less value but is an easier entry for folks who have more limited budgets.

- **But what if they're a nonprofit or a startup with no money?** Tough. Do you think the power company is charging them less because of who they are? Nope. So why should you? If they can't afford you, then they'll have to go elsewhere. And if they really want to afford you, they'll find a way to do it, either by finding more money somewhere or by changing the work (maybe you create a template for the newsletter rather than designing the whole thing). You are not running a charity service.

- **But they say they have lots more work to send me after we do this first one cheap!** Baloney. Maybe they're the one-in-a-million client who actually does have more work coming, but if you do it cheap now, they're going to want it cheap later too. Don't kid yourself that they're magically going to be happy to pay you more after this.
- **But it's my good friend. Shouldn't I give her a discount?** Definitely not. Especially not. (See the earlier section on working with friends and family.) Your friends and family should know how good you are at what you do and want to support you and see you succeed. So they should actually pay more. But definitely not less. Discounts breed resentment, which is definitely something you want to avoid with family and friends.
- **They don't have any money, but they can trade me for xyz.** It can be tempting to work for trade, but don't do it. Even if it's something you really want or think you'll use, just say no. It's messy and doesn't pay the bills, and I'm sure there are tax reasons not to (that's not for me to say). In the past, I've traded design work for massages, a painting, and even a week at a cabin in Tahoe. Guess how many of those things I've actually gotten or used? Yeah, none. Which means I worked for free, even though we had the best of intentions.
- **But what if I'm just starting out or times are tough and I *really* need the work?** If you really need the work, then that's your good reason to discount your prices. When times get tough, some money is better than no money at all. I know lots of folks who lowered their rates a bit during the height of the pandemic when business slowed to a crawl and they needed to keep the lights on. It happens. It can be really hard to stick to your guns and charge your full rate when you don't have enough work. I've been there too. But reduce your rates consciously and on purpose. And let clients know that they're getting a special rate from you, framed in a way that makes them feel like you're doing them a favor rather than you needing the work. So instead of telling them that you're discounting the project because you're slow, tell them you're offering a "pandemic discount" or a "new client discount" or whatever makes sense in the moment. If you make it clear that they're getting a reduced rate, that also lets them know that your usual rate is higher and helps sets expectations for future projects. Your lowered rate should be temporary.

Remember, there's an opportunity cost to lowering your rates. If you take on lower paying work, you'll be booked up when the higher paying work comes along. Most people don't consider this in the heat of the moment.

Never work for free

People who tell you they'll have more work if you do this one for free are lying. Even if they think they are telling the truth, even if their intentions are good, they're not going to want to pay—and pay well—for something they've already gotten for free. Free work takes time away from your paying clients and other marketing that you could be doing to get real work. Free work devalues your skill, time, and effort. You are a professional.

Never work for exposure either. Just because other people will see your work, doesn't mean they'll care who did it or want to hire you. Eyeballs and views don't pay rent.

What about pro bono work?

Pro bono work is a different beast, but still a fancy way of saying *free*. Personally, I think it's OK to do it every now and then if you're really clear about why you're doing it. Generally it should be done as part of a larger marketing strategy (i.e. you can use this free project as an example to get in the door somewhere bigger) or as your way of volunteering for an organization you care about.

For the past three years, I've served on the board of the PTA at my son's school, and I do a few pro bono projects a year for them—a big fundraiser in the fall and then a few flyers throughout the year. I'm generally happy to do them because I know my work is directly supporting the school. I don't put my full effort into any of those projects. My "good enough" is fine, and usually far better than what they would have gotten from the neighbor's wife's nephew anyway. I do enough that I can be proud of the results and feel good about helping the school without spending a ton of time on it. And then I can use those project samples to help me market to other school districts so that I can get paid to do the work that I love. For me it's a win-win.

When possible, the receiver of your free efforts should be actively participating so that they're doing work for free too. Maybe they write the copy, research and provide all of the sponsor logos, or find the images they want to use. Share the load a bit and get everyone invested in the project.

TAKE THE
Next Step

GOOD

- ☐ Say your hourly rate out loud. "I charge $XXX per hour." Get comfortable with it.
- ☐ Write down three scenarios in which you might consider doing something pro bono, and why it might benefit you.

GOOD

- ☐ Have some scripts on hand so you know what to say if someone questions your rate.
- ☐ Stop doing any work that you're currently not being paid for or at least set an end date.

BEST

- ☐ Get comfortable with the fact that some clients will not be able to afford you. That's good.
- ☐ Say no to the next person who asks for something free.

NOTES

Invoice consistently.

If you don't send an invoice, you don't get paid. Period. Figure out what works for you based on your project type and workload—that might be at the end of each project or milestone, or every two weeks, or every month. Whatever that is, make it happen. If you don't take care of your business finances, you won't have a business for very long.

Paperwork is a lot less fun than whatever else you're doing, but it's important. I personally hate invoicing. Sometimes I do it at the end of a particular project, and that's quick and easy to do. But I do the bulk of my invoicing at the end of every month because I do quite a bit of ongoing hourly work. It's tedious and takes several hours to add up all of the time between me and my contractors, but I do it—even if it means that I'm doing it on a Friday night or over a weekend. Don't get me wrong—hours of invoicing is a great problem to have, and I'm grateful for that. But if I could figure out how to pass it off to someone else I would.

Depending on your number and type of clients or projects, invoicing once might not be enough to keep a regular flow of cash. Without the steady paycheck of an outside job, cash flow can be an issue. Your bank account might be empty one minute and flush with cash the next. You can minimize the fluctuations a bit by staggering client payments and invoicing in smaller chunks more frequently. You might consider milestone payments (payments due at particular points during the project), but beware—if the project gets stalled at any point, you'll be stuck. This has happened to me more than once, often during web design projects. I used to set up payment schedules to have a milestone payment due at the end of the design phase, which seemed reasonable. But then I would run into situations where the client would put the project aside for a few months, or delay sending final approval on the design, or increase the scope a bit, all of which delayed my ability to invoice on that milestone. A better option, and what I now do instead, especially for longer-term projects, is to have set payments due at regular intervals. That way I can invoice whether the project is on schedule or not, and my cash flow stays steady.

How should you invoice? That's up to you—there are a lot of great options out there. FreshBooks and QuickBooks seem to be the most popular with my colleagues and contractors. I use FileMaker Pro to create the invoices, and then send them off as PDFs to my clients (my bookkeeper enters them into QuickBooks later). Others just send PDFs done by hand in Excel; just make sure all the needed information is on there—the project, rate, total, and information about how, where, and when to pay.

Always get a deposit

Yes, *always*. A deposit gets the client invested in the project, minimizes your risk of not getting anything if the project goes sideways, and makes you look like a professional. Most businesses require a deposit or payment up front, and so should you. You can decide for yourself if and when to break that rule, but make it a rule. Especially with clients that you've never worked with before. Most creatives I know ask for 50 percent up front (before work begins) and 50 percent upon final delivery. If it's a longer-term project with a big budget, you might ask for 25 percent up front and the rest spread out over the course of the engagement at set intervals.

Sometimes getting a deposit can be tricky. Many of my clients at larger organizations take up to thirty days to cut and send a check, and we don't often have an extra thirty days before the project needs to start, so I have to decide whether to take it on faith that they'll pay or push back on the timing. Sometimes a project will be completed in a matter of days or weeks, long before a deposit check would arrive. For clients I trust, it's a no-brainer for me to get started without having the deposit in hand or to waive it altogether if the project is completed quickly. If it's someone I've never worked for before, then they either need to find a way to pay the deposit faster, or I have a tough decision to make.

What happens if they don't pay?

Unfortunately, this will happen at some point to most of us. I've been burned several times, for big money, and it sucks.

The best offense is a good defense. Keep the issue from happening in the first place by having a good contract, requiring a down payment, and not delivering final files until you have the money. That works well for individuals and smaller clients, but prompt payment can be difficult with some larger organizations that need to go through accounting channels, so you can't always hold things hostage while you wait (unless you don't want to work for that client again).

So what are your options if they aren't paying?

1. **Nag them.** By phone, by email, whatever. Be a pest. A professional, courteous, pest. Most of the time, I find that a simple email reminder is all it takes to get a check cut. Keep your cool, and remember that the person cutting the check may not actually be the person in charge of the money—this is especially true in a larger organization. If they're close by, show up at the office and ask in person. Preeti is a CAD designer, and when she doesn't get paid, she shows up at her client's door with her in-

voice every day until they pay her. "I once had to visit a client every day for a week until I got paid. Luckily it's rare, but I want them to see that they're dealing with a real person and not just an email. It's harder for them to keep putting me off when I'm right in their face." I'm not sure I could do this, although if the check was big enough maybe I could. If you're conflict-averse like me, have someone else nag them. My book-keeper is great at this.

2. **Withhold delivery.** Depending on the deliverables, demand cash on receipt. Don't load any website files until the check is in the bank. Don't send the final copy or logos until they've paid. I once had a client who was really delinquent on a final payment for a website, so I pulled down the site and told her I'd reload it once she paid. I don't know that I would do that again today, but it worked. One of my web developer colleagues (no one I ever collaborated with) used to secretly put a line of "kill code" into every website he built, and if the invoice wasn't paid by a certain date, the code would activate and break the site. If the client paid on time, he would log in to the server and remove it. I don't recommend that on ethical or logistical grounds, but sometimes creative measures are needed when it comes to getting paid.

3. **Stop working.** If you're partway through a project and aren't getting paid your deposit or a milestone payment, stop working. Don't waste your time on work if they're not respecting the agreement they made with you.

4. **Sue them.** You can sue or threaten to sue, but taking someone to small-claims court is time-consuming and expensive for everyone. I once had a festival client stiff me for thousands of dollars at the end of a project and nagging wasn't working. So I tried to take her to small-claims court. I sent her a registered letter to start the process, but she wouldn't accept it, so in the end I just had to ...

5. **Let it go.** Sometimes you just have to let it go before it consumes you. Is the money worth the time and mental effort it's going to take to get it? Do they even have the money to give you? If not, chalk it up to a lesson learned. Sometimes life just happens too. One of my clients died unexpectedly with some of my invoices unpaid, and I just let them go. The thought of contacting a grieving husband about a relatively small amount of money didn't feel good to me, and I could afford to go without. On the flip side, one of my colleagues was doing some interior design work for a client that she knew had a terminal disease, and as the client got sicker, they talked about payment with her spouse ahead of her passing so he wouldn't be surprised.

I always say that the biggest lessons I've learned have cost me money, although it might just be that those lessons are the most painful. When it does happen, take a good hard look at the situation and figure out what you could have done differently, if anything, and use that to guide you moving forward. While these hard lessons are inevitable, most clients pay on time and pay well, and those who are late generally feel bad about it and rectify the situation as soon as you remind them. I've never gone hungry waiting on an outstanding invoice. So in the end, it all works out.

TAKE THE Next Step

GOOD

☐ Get a deposit on your next project.
☐ Invoice at least once a month.

BETTER

☐ Look at last month's invoices to see who hasn't paid yet. Follow up with those clients.
☐ Look at your cash flow and consider how you might be able to adjust your payment schedules.

BEST

☐ Hire a bookkeeper to do your invoicing and follow up with overdue payments.
☐ Look at your financial statements monthly.

Save money for taxes and emergencies.

Now that you're getting paid, you need to be thinking ahead to tax time (bleh, I know). April 15 might feel *really* far away, but it'll be here faster than you think. There's nothing worse than a surprise at tax time, and I know about this firsthand.

I'd been in business for myself for three years, and things were rolling along swimmingly. I was making good money and was incredibly busy. Too busy, in fact, to think about taxes, or budgeting, or setting aside money—I just threw my money in the bank and figured I had enough for taxes later on. Wrong. I hadn't been in business long enough or made enough money to be paying quarterly taxes yet, so I got hit with a $40K tax bill. I was stunned. And I didn't have that much money in the bank.

I was fortunate that my dad, who is also self-employed, understood what I was going through and was generous enough to loan me the $10K I didn't have. I paid him back over the course of the following months and vowed never to let that happen again—and to never be surprised like that as well.

The IRS forced me to pay quarterly after that, which helped me stay on top of tax payments. I hired an accountant and handed over my tax prep (that one felt good!). I hired a bookkeeper so that I always knew how I was doing financially and paid more attention to what was coming in and what was going out. And I saved 40 percent of every check I got so that I'd have some buffer moving forward.

I've heard people say that you should save up to 50 percent of every check. That can be hard to do when you're just starting out and not making very much. But unless you have a healthy cushion to fall back on, it's really important to save at least 25 percent, especially if you're on your own and don't have a partner or spouse's income to support yours. Eventually you can beef that up as you're making more so that you have plenty saved for taxes and also as a rainy day fund in case work slows down or a partner gets laid off. My husband has been laid off a few times over the years, and each time I was grateful that we had four month's worth of savings on hand. It made me feel a little less panicked and anxious as he hunted for a new position.

Another benefit to socking money away? *Freedom.* Freedom to be able to quit the part-time job and work for yourself full-time. Freedom from worry and anxiety when you have a slow month. Freedom to fire that client that you're not crazy about and have some buffer while you find the right one. Freedom to be choosy about the work you say yes to. Freedom to take time off, remodel your house, donate to causes you believe in, or take that dream vacation. Freedom to support yourself if something goes awry with a business or romantic partner. And yes, freedom to know that if an emergency pops up, you're prepared financially.

For a creative person, being an entrepreneur is the ultimate freedom. Not only can we do the work we want to do, but we can create the environment and the circumstances in which we do it. And the more money we have at our disposal, the more flexibility we have to create the life we want. Creative entrepreneurs start their businesses for any number of reasons, but at the most basic level we want to be paid to create the work that excites us and have the time and space to do whatever that is. Most of the creative business owners I know are creating *all the time*. My friend Julie loves tending her garden, cooking exotic meals, and painting when she's not doing design work. My friend Gigi writes books and hosts a podcast when she's not coaching her public speaking clients.

TAKE THE Next Step

GOOD

☐ Set aside 25 percent of every check you get and put it somewhere you can't touch unless it's an emergency. Use it to pay your taxes.

BETTER

☐ Look at your overall finances and set a budget. Set aside money for taxes and put anything else you don't spend into savings.

BEST

☐ Pay your taxes quarterly and keep three to six months of expenses in a savings account.

Save money for retirement.

Eventually, hopefully, sooner rather than later, you'll want to think about retirement. The more you can sock away now, the better off you'll be down the road. How you save will depend on variables like your business structure, desire for risk, and how much you have to invest.

Retirement plans can be confusing, and it can be a challenge to know what kind of account you should have based on your business type. You'll likely have a SIMPLE IRA (individual retirement account), a SEP IRA, a traditional or Roth IRA, or a solo 401(k). Each of those account types has different rules, so an accountant or financial planner can help you sort out which options are best for you. You can also contact many of the big investing companies (like Charles Schwab or Fidelity) and ask for recommendations and advice at no charge.

I had the good fortune to have a boss in my previous life who set up an IRA for me as part of my benefits package, so I transferred that when I went out on my own and continued making contributions. When I became an S corp three years ago, I converted that IRA to a solo 401(k) based on my new company status and my advisor's advice.

When should you contribute?

That depends. When I first started out, I had no idea how much money I would make in a year, and what that would mean for contribution limits (or how much cash I would have saved up to actually make the contribution). So every year my accountant would tell me what I owed in taxes and what a contribution might do to that number, and I'd decide what to do from there. I didn't always contribute as much as I would have liked to, but I still contributed something. By the time I incorporated, my yearly income was pretty steady, so I had a good idea of what I could contribute, but I still chose to make one deposit mid-year and another at tax-time just to be sure. Writing large checks is a bit of a bummer, so this year I automated the process and have part of every paycheck automatically deposited in my 401(k). I don't have to think about it, and if my income suddenly drops, I can always make changes.

How much should you contribute?

There's no one right answer to that either. Ideally, you're maxing out whatever accounts you have (there are limits to how much the IRS will allow you to contribute each year to certain types of accounts), but start with whatever you can.

Not sure how much you can sock away or what type of account you should have? The IRS website is a great place to start—they've got an easy-to-navigate section on retirement plans and contribution limits: https://www.irs.gov/retirement-plans. Sites like NerdWallet and any of the big investing companies like Schwab and Fidelity have lots of information as well. A visit with an accountant can help you decide what plan works best for you from a tax perspective, how much money you can afford to set aside, and how much you're allowed to set aside based on your age and income.

If you're opening a new account, there are lots of companies out there that make it really easy to start investing with little money or know-how. Here are just a few, not endorsed by me—you'll need to research them for yourself: Schwab, Fidelity, TIAA, Mint, or NerdWallet. Or consider asking friends and colleagues for recommendations.

Do you need to use a financial planner for yourself?

No. But it might be helpful. Lots of financial companies have free accounts and access to planners who can answer questions as they come up. You might also have the time and interest to learn about investments and figure out your own plan, but I don't really have either of those things. I love being able to tell my planner what my goals are or ask for a recommendation, and then have her take care of it. The trade-off is that I have to pay for that service, but the time and mental space it frees up for me are totally worth it.

Do you need to hire a financial advisor for the business?

No. But depending on the size of your company and your goals, it might be a good idea. I've never done it, but a colleague of mine started a small marketing company last year and hired a consultant to help her figure out how much she could afford in salaries, contractor fees, and other business expenses in order to meet her goals and stay profitable. That sort of ongoing expense feels like a lot to me, at least right now. I prefer to ask my accountant when I have questions and talk to other creatives I know to see how they're growing their businesses, and then see what feels right to me. But I can definitely see value in hiring someone else to figure out the details, tell me what they think I should do, and give me a plan to follow.

TAKE THE
Next Step

☑ ☑

☐ Pick a set amount of money for retirement that works with your budget and set it aside in a savings account that you don't touch. Put something in it every month, even if it's only a few dollars at a time.

BETTER

☐ Pick an investment company and set up an IRA—they'll help you. Talk to an accountant and find out what you can contribute each month based on your income.

BEST

☐ Set up an automatic monthly contribution from your bank account into your IRA. Transfer the max amount if you can or play it safe and transfer a lower amount monthly, capped off by an additional contribution at the end of the year.

NOTES

I HAVE *not* FAILED. I'VE JUST FOUND 10,000 WAYS THAT *won't* WORK

— THOMAS A. EDISON

Mistakes will be made, and plans will go sideways. But that's a good thing! It means that lessons will be learned, and you'll be smarter and better able to tackle similar situations down the road. Let's talk about some of the pitfalls that might arise and what to do about them.

DO GOOD WORK

Prioritize customer service— within reason.

Throughout my business life, I've made a point to learn what it means to serve customers well. I used to have a client who would introduce me as "The Nordstrom of Designers" (or "The Zappos of Designers" for the younger readers) because of my amazing customer service. Always available, always pleasant, always helpful.

The payoff of good customer services is that a happy client keeps coming back and tells all of their friends about you. But there are some limits to the formula for success and riches. If you offer one specific type of service that tends to be one and done, like a wedding video, then you likely won't have repeat clients (unless you work in Hollywood or Vegas). Customers might not have friends or colleagues who need the service you offer, and if you're not marketing yourself and reminding them that you exist, they might not remember you down the road. But if you're occasionally keeping in touch and gave them a great customer experience, you'll greatly increase your chances of working with or selling to them again or getting a great referral. Plus, good customer service tends to make projects go smoothly.

What does good customer service even mean? I've found over the years that it depends—good customer service is whatever your customers think it is. It's whatever it takes to solve your customer's problems in a way that meets the needs of your business.

There are no definitive lists, but, in general, here are a few things good customer service is.

- **Timely.** Most people don't expect an immediate response when they contact you, but they don't expect to wait days for a response—unless you set that expectation up front via a voicemail greeting or automated email message. I can't tell you how many times I've responded to an email from someone new, even if it's several hours after they reached out to me, and am greeted with surprise and gratitude that I responded so fast.
- **Clear.** When I hire someone to do a job for me, I want to know the details: What it will cost, when I can expect things to happen, how often they'll update me, and how I can reach them. If they have specific methods or schedules for communication, I want to know—even if it's not as quick or responsive as I would like. At least if I know what to expect and can rely on it, I can decide if it works for me.
- **Convenient and accessible.** Good customer service is easy to find and use in a variety of formats. Make sure your customers can find and reach you easily. If you've got forms on your website, make them easy to understand and navigate. Have clear calls to action and graphics that are easy to navigate and use. Don't make people jump through hoops to work with you—they're probably not gonna do that. For example, a while back, I had an issue with my website domain and needed to get information from the registration company. When I went to their website, I discovered there was no way to get in touch with tech support, other than to fill out a form and wait forty-eight hours for a response. No phone number, no online chat, nothing. As soon as I found my answer, I pulled my business and moved to another company that was easier to get a hold of, with a phone number and chat line clearly listed and available.
- **Personalized.** Everyone wants to feel appreciated. Good customer service makes people feel valued and like their business matters, even for the smallest projects. It's friendly and helpful and fosters connection, even when things go wrong.
- **Proactive.** Resolving potential problems at the first sign of trouble is good service. If new products or systems become available that would benefit a client, let them know about it. Being proactive reinforces that

you're thinking about the particular needs of the people you work with and paying attention.

It doesn't take all that much effort to give good service, but lots of other businesses don't. So it's relatively easy to give your existing and potential customers a great experience from the start. Let them know what to expect, where and when to reach you, and that you care. Pretty soon they'll be calling you the Nordstrom or Zappos of whatever it is you do.

Customer service is about focusing on their needs first, but to do that well you need to know—and be comfortable with—your own limitations. Setting boundaries doesn't limit your ability to provide good service; it actually protects your skills and resources so that you can continually offer the best service.

As most new entrepreneurs are tempted to do, Kevin Mercier viewed every new customer as the lifeline to keep his photography and travel blog business afloat—it was only natural to feel inclined to bend over backward to make every new customer as happy as possible. "On the whole, this was a good impulse. But at the same time, I was making the mistake of not keeping any limits. Soon after, I had to deal with customers making unreasonable requests. The problem with granting those requests was that they came to haunt me later because they had set precedents that were difficult to undo. After two years, I realized that it was necessary to set boundaries with each customer early on to define the relationship. I concluded that if our products and services had real value, the customer would understand those boundaries and stick with me. If they didn't, then it was probably a good idea to let them be someone else's headache."

Here are a few things that you *don't* have to be.

- **You don't have to be perfect.** Nobody is perfect, and you're not going to get it right all the time, even if you're trying your hardest. Even with the best of intentions, you're going to forget to turn your phone ringer on one morning or be forty-five minutes late to a meeting because you can't find parking. As long as you're making the effort to give the best service you reasonably can, apologizing for errors when you need to, and being up front about limitations and expectations, your customers will appreciate it.
- **You don't have to drop everything for them or respond immediately.** I once had the audacity to go to the supermarket in the afternoon—it's one of the benefits of running your own business. One of my retainer clients called me as I was walking into the store. He asked me if I could update a newsletter we were working on and send it back to him. I actually turned around and drove right home, updated the newsletter,

and emailed him before going back to the store that night. Did he ask me to do it right now? No. Would he have been just as appreciative if he'd gotten it once I'd done my shopping? Yes. Who was the idiot that thought that being a good vendor meant being at my desk for every single minute of the workday? Me. Don't be like me.

- **You are not a doormat.** Just because someone is paying you money for something, or wants to pay you for something, doesn't mean that they own you or get to micromanage you or dictate how you spend your time. If you do have an overly demanding client who is pushing against the boundaries you've set for yourself and project, here are a few things you can do.

  → If the project hasn't started yet, and the prospect is already being demanding in some way, like asking for an unreasonable rush, you can say no or offer an alternative that does work for you. I have a client that I've worked with for years who is *always* in a rush. She routinely sends me an email with the details for a poster she needs, due the next day, and assumes that I'll just take care of it. Sometimes I can, but as my business grows, I often can't just drop everything else (or don't have the free time in my schedule) to squeeze it in. So I've started pushing back, politely of course. I tell her that "I can't get this done for you tomorrow, but I can get it done for you on [date]. Will that work?" Then she has the option of saying yes or no and either gives me the time I need or takes that emergency elsewhere. How she responds varies on the situation. Sometimes we compromise somewhere in between, sometimes I charge her a rush fee and have a contractor handle it for me, and sometimes she ends up finding another solution if I really can't help her. We've known each other long enough that me pushing back isn't a deal-breaker.

  → If a client you're working with is being unreasonable but you're open to continuing the relationship, an uncomfortable conversation is in order. Set a meeting with them and have a conversation to remind them about the boundaries you've already set—or even set new boundaries. Be explicit about what you need, whether that's a minimum turnaround time for all projects or hefty rush fees or fewer phone calls. Let them know specifically what they're doing that isn't working for you and what needs to change. Ask them if there's something they feel they need from you in order to make the relationship work—the conversation can be a two-way street. Once the air is clear, you can decide if you want to continue the relationship or let them go.

  → In my experience, it has always been pretty clear when it was time to let a client go. At some point, I just know in my gut that whatever isn't working isn't getting better and likely isn't going to. The few times that's happened to me, we were close enough to the end the whatever project we were working on that I stuck it out, wrapped it up, and didn't work with them again. If someone was really violating a boundary or abusing me in some way, I would end it immediately. Thankfully that hasn't happened so far.

The customer is not the boss of you—they really aren't. You don't have to put up with ridiculous demands or behavior to make people happy. Standing up for yourself protects you and your business so that you can enjoy your work and keep offering good service—to that client or the clients to come.

TAKE THE Next Step

GOOD

☐ Make sure your preferred method of contact is listed clearly on your website and materials.

BETTER

☐ Return emails and phone calls within twenty-four hours.

BEST

☐ Check in with ongoing clients weekly to give a quick update in between any scheduled meetings. Mention any potential red flags you see coming up and what you're doing to monitor the situation.

Communicate openly and honestly.

No matter who you're talking to, open and honest communication is a must. Telling the truth can be really scary. Whether you need to be vulnerable and fess up to something, or if you're on the other side and need to tell someone else that something they're doing isn't cutting it—just say it nicely. Anything else results in wasted time and mucks up what could otherwise be a great experience or relationship.

Good communication skills don't always come naturally, but they can be learned and improved through practice. If you struggle, here are some ways you can improve your skills.

- **Be clear and concise when you speak.** Use straightforward language, avoid the jargon, and get to the point. Provide enough specific information for understanding and avoid rambling.
- **Practice active listening.** Pay attention when your conversation partner is speaking, and focus on listening attentively rather than simply waiting to say your response. Ask clarifying questions, avoid interrupting, and repeat key points to make sure you've understood the message.
- **Pay attention to nonverbal cues, both yours and theirs.** Make eye contact, and keep in mind that body language, tone, and facial expressions convey messages too.
- **Consider your audience.** Tailor your communication style accordingly. I'm generally a believer in speaking kindly and carefully, or "catching more flies with honey than vinegar." My husband on the other hand is brutally honest and direct with the people he manages, a style which works for him and totally doesn't work for me.
- **Eliminate distractions.** Put away the phone or email so that you can focus on the person you're speaking to.
- **Prepare ahead of time and practice.** Organize your thoughts, prepare a script with what you want to say, and anticipate questions or pushback. Have responses ready so that you don't have to react on the fly.
- **Get clarification.** Not sure what someone means by something they said or a nonverbal cue they're exhibiting? Ask questions! "What did you mean by x?" "Are you saying y?" "I'm hearing you say x, but am sensing y by the look on your face, so can you tell me more?"

Open communication doesn't necessarily need to be a bad thing either. Good relationships are built on mutual trust and understanding, so the clearer you can be about everything, the better it is for everyone. So don't be chicken. Say what you need to say.

TAKE THE
Next Step

☑ ☑

GOOD

☐ Write down a script for a conversation you need to have.

BETTER

☐ Practice what you want to say, either by yourself or with a partner.

BEST

☐ Have the conversation, calmly and matter-of-factly.

Say "I don't know," then find out.

Whether someone is asking about a skill you don't have or when something will happen or what something will cost, if you don't know the answer or aren't fully confident about it, be honest. Don't guess (you'll be wrong) or try to bullshit your way through it (they'll smell you coming a mile away). All you have to say is: "Good question. I don't know, but I'll find out/figure it out and get back to you." They're not expecting you to know everything; they're expecting you to be honest and resourceful.

If a potential or new client is in an industry you're not familiar with and using jargon you don't understand, say so. Ask them to tell you more about x, y, and z or explain a bit more about what they mean by something. We can't know everything, and maybe we do actually know what they're talking about but would call it something else. A good client will be more than happy to tell you more and explain something to you, especially since it means you'll understand what they're talking about after that. People tend to enjoy talking about their work, especially with someone who's inquisitive and listens well. Even if you think it's something you should know, ask anyway (or at the very least, look it up later). Much better to ask a question than to make a mistake.

Be honest about what you don't know, but focus on what you've done that is similar or other skills you have that are complementary or applicable. How can what you've done before translate into something they need? Maybe you've worked in a totally different industry, but the problem you solved is the same. Maybe the prospect wants an annual report, but you worked on a book that also had charts and graphs in it. Maybe they're looking for event graphics, but you've done a fundraising invitation suite with some of the same types of pieces with a consistently designed suite of materials.

Guessing or making it up as you go will bite you in the ass. I promise. Do your homework, figure out who does know what you don't, and get the answers from them. This has come up for me a few times, especially when it comes to work that I have some familiarity with but don't do myself, like copywriting and web development. I remember one time in particular when I was on an initial call with a prospect for a web project. I asked about a few of the new features she wanted to incorporate and what her budget looked like, and she told me that another firm she'd talked to had quoted her $20K and that she thought that was high. I also thought it was high and told her I expected that our bid would be much lower than that. I was wrong. After talking through the scope with the developer, our estimate was very close to that $20K number, and I had to go back to the prospect and explain why my quote was so much higher than I had expected. It didn't feel great to me to be wrong, and it may have made me a less than ideal vendor for her (we didn't get the job).

Get over imposter syndrome

Even though I've been doing this business and design thing for a while and generally know what I'm talking about, I still have bouts of imposter syndrome. Before every meeting with a new prospect or client, I have flashes of doubt. I've learned over time to acknowledge that fear, and then push it to the side. Because even if any of those things happen, so what? People make mistakes. You don't know everything. But you are resilient, and you can learn.

- **Will I sound like an idiot?** Probably not. Most clients want to hire you to do a job they know little or nothing about, so frankly you could say just about anything, and they would take your word for it, especially if you say it with confidence. They're calling you because they need your guidance. Even if they're in your field and have an understanding of what you do, they either can't do it themselves or don't have time to do it. And there are different ways of completing the same project, so even if they know how to do the job and would do it differently than you, say what you know, and you'll be fine.
- **What if I make a mistake about something I should know?** So what? Correct yourself or acknowledge the correction and move on. If a prospect or client is a jerk about that, then you probably don't want to work for them anyway.
- **What if I don't understand the terminology they're using?** Easy. Ask them to clarify. Or say, "Tell me more about that." You might even look smart and curious in the process.
- **What if I can't answer a question they have?** Again, not the end of the world. As we touched on earlier, don't bullshit your way through it—be honest and say that you don't know the answer, say what you do know, and then tell them how and when you'll have that answer. This happens to me all the time with web projects. I'm not a developer, so I can speak to the general things that I know and refer specific or technical questions to the people who actually have the answers. Not knowing something is fine, as long as you then say that you'll find out.

Even if you're not feeling confident, fake it and speak with authority (without being an asshole, of course). Nobody has to know that you're quaking inside or feeling like a fraud. You're better than you think you are, and eventually your mind will catch up.

TAKE THE
Next Step

☑ ☑

GOOD

☐ If you're not sure what something means, ask.
☐ Stay curious and listen closely to find out what other people need.

BETTER

☐ Instead of bluffing your way through a situation, tell the client/prospect that you need to look into that and will get back to them.

BEST

☐ Have resources at the ready that you can call on for answers, advice, or even to refer.

NOTES

Learn to love saying no.

I do not like conflict, and I try to avoid it as much as I can. For most of my life, this has meant saying yes to just about everything, even if it's something I'd rather not do. In business, I said yes 99.9 percent of the time, especially at first. I took just about every project and client that came my way, even if the money was bad or the client or project not a good fit.

As someone trying to get a fledgling business off the ground, that was totally understandable. But I kept saying yes to everything throughout the years. On the rare occasions where I turned down a project, I felt really bad about it.

My usual response was to say yes, even if budgets were too low (I can work fast!) or the turnaround was too tight (panic of my own making is fun!) or I already had work on my plate (who needs sleep anyway!). I always said yes so that I could be the hero and make clients like me and not have to say no.

But what I didn't realize until much later is that saying yes to something also means that you're saying no to something else, even if it's not explicitly said. Maybe that yes means that you're saying no to spending time with your family. Maybe it's saying no to getting enough sleep and taking care of yourself. Maybe it's saying no to feeling relaxed and happy.

If you want to say yes to something, by all means do. But do it consciously and be aware of what you're giving up (or saying no to) in return. Make sure the trade-off is worth it.

Jeanine Davis of JL Davis Design had no problem saying no to an early marketing client who asked her to reduce her hourly rate in return for a lot more work. "He thought he was dangling the juicy carrot of more work to entice me to say yes, but why on earth would I want to spend more time working for less money? What kind of reward is that?"

Rodika Tollefson, owner of nMeta Communications, Inc. is a technology and cybersecurity content writer and strategist who stopped working with an ongoing client after they hired a new content manager who was not ideal to work with. "They wanted to get on a call to go over their self-explanatory edits and just randomly emailed me to ask if I could hop on a call now, that sort of thing. After we finished the project, the manager asked if anyone on my team specialized in their exact (very niche) topic so they could hire us for another project. Rather than checking with my network to see if I could find other writers who knew the subject deeper, I said no. It was not worth the headache. I would have loved to go back to that company for more projects and kept watching to see if that person moved on, but they didn't so eventually I filed them under 'past clients.'"

I still struggle with saying no, but I'm getting a lot better at it, and I don't feel bad anymore. Saying no in a few key instances this year has made all the difference in my mental health and my ability to get a little bit of balance in my life. I've taken some chunks of time off this year and got requests for rush work right before I left. I said no, and they either used another vendor or waited for me to come back. The fear that I might lose the client forever by turning down work in favor of my vacation was still there, but I know I can't control what anyone else does regardless of what I say or do. So I ignore that people-pleasing inner voice and trust that saying no is the right thing to do for me in that moment.

Be generous with referrals

A few times a year, I get calls about projects that aren't a good fit for me. Maybe they're too small, a type of work I can't (or don't want to) do, or don't work for me in terms of timing. When that happens I love being able to refer my colleagues. I used to look at those projects in terms of money lost and might have even tried to make them happen on my own, but now I look at them in terms what is gained by being generous and suggesting someone else. There is plenty of work for everyone, and when I refer things that aren't right for me instead of wasting my time doing something I can't or don't want to do, I'm freeing up space for the right work to come in.

The colleague I'm referring gets work. The prospect or client who called gets help. I get the satisfaction of knowing that I facilitated that and that my time is free to do other things. It's a win for everyone. And karma has a way of swinging back around in one way or another. I benefit from referrals, so I want to help others get them too.

Generosity also pays in general. That might mean simply answering a question or giving advice, or giving a referral for something that has nothing to do with work. That might look like sharing my printing contacts with clients who need to get something printed, even if I wasn't involved in the project and don't get a cut of the cost; sharing a parenting book I read or a podcast I listened to a colleague struggling with their kids; recommending the painters we used for a client who is redecorating her office; answering a question about InDesign or giving a website tutorial to a client so that they can update their new website themselves; or sharing my experience with a vendor in a networking group.

Generosity can be really simple and take no time at all. If the offering you can make is larger in scope and is something you're typically paid for, then mention that—maybe there's a way to give a taste of it or give a quick fix for free and then transition that to something paid. And even if it's not work-related, being generous with your time and knowledge positions you as someone who can help and who has the answers—someone that people can rely on. And maybe even someone who they'll want to work with when the next project rolls around.

TAKE THE
Next Step

GOOD

☐ Before you say your next yes, take a moment to consider what you're also saying no to.

BETTER

☐ Say no to a project or client that doesn't feel right and have a few scripts ready if you need them.

☐ Compile a list of referral sources and trusted vendors and keep it handy.

BEST

☐ Say no and offer an alternative solution if you like. Otherwise just say no and leave it at that.

NOTES

Get everybody in the room.

Now that you have a foundation for strong communication, have the right people in the room—your team and theirs—especially in the beginning. Everyone involved in the project will be looking at it through a different lens and will have different things they need to know and different things to share. Kicking off a meeting about a new brochure? Make sure the copywriter is there too. When you're meeting about that big website project, the designer and developer should both be there.

It might feel like a pain to involve more people, but not having the information you need (or worse, the wrong information) is an even bigger pain. For everyone. Instead of bogging down the process, having extra time for clear communication at the beginning helps the process go smoothly.

Bring your team into the conversation. I was working on a website project for a new client that involved setting up email, which is usually a really simple thing. It never occurred to me that setting up the mail in a certain software product wasn't so simple, and I had no idea that I even needed to ask about that. Had the developer been in the room with me, she would have asked about that and understood what was involved, and it would have saved us both a lot of heartburn and money moving forward.

Make sure the client is bringing the right people too. As you talk with a prospective client, get a sense of the overall scope and ask questions to figure out what work will need to be done and who needs to be involved. Then get those people on the next call to really ask questions and nail down the scope. If you're getting the sense that someone isn't included who should be, ask. I've worked on a few projects where the client has their own copywriter, social media poster, or web developer, and those folks are never included in my meetings with the client. In those cases, I try to at least have some sort of quick introductory email or phone call so that we're at least familiar with each other and are available to answer questions or make adjustments as we go.

That said, there can definitely be too many cooks in the kitchen once everyone is in the room. The more voices you have, the more complicated things can get, especially if they're not all in agreement. So, even though you want to hear what different people have to say, make sure there is one single point of contact on both sides. There should be one person in charge of the project on the client side, who will manage any internal disagreements and wrangle all feedback so that you're getting a single set of comments. There's nothing worse than getting one set of notes from one contact and getting a conflicting set of comments from another. Who do you listen to then? (More on that in the next section.) On your side, there should be a single voice as well. If I'm partnering with a developer on a project, the lead is the person who brought in the project. That doesn't mean that the other partner is not visible or able to speak, but it generally means that they sit back and let the other person be the main point of contact and lead the conversation.

TAKE THE
Next Step

GOOD

☐ Figure out who you need on your team for your next project, either in advance or on a discovery call.

BETTER

☐ Include your key team members on a call so that they can ask questions and help determine the full scope of the project.

BEST

☐ Include everyone in the conversation, but pick one point of contact for your team and agree on a single point of contact for the client team.

Learn the art of feedback.

Giving and getting feedback is likely an integral part of your job. On rare occasions the client loves the work that you did or agrees with and approves your recommendations immediately. But most of the time there are at least some (hopefully minor) edits to make or discussions to be had before you wrap up and say goodbye to a satisfied client.

Feedback is a two-way street. The client has some responsibility to give it well, and you have the responsibility make sure you're getting what you need and receiving it well.

- **Be specific about what you want feedback on and how and when.** Do you need the client to choose one option and comment on specific parts of it (fonts, color, tone of voice, etc.), or do you need more general overarching feedback? Are you looking for nitty-gritty text and grammar edits or feedback on the basic concept? If you want to review it via phone, get something scheduled. If you want them to mark up a PDF or type up edits in a Word doc, tell them. If you're on a schedule, give them a deadline and let them know what happens if they miss it. If you don't have a specific deadline to meet, set one anyway. The clearer you are about what kind of feedback you need and how and when you want it, the more likely you are to get what you need.
- **Choose a single point of contact, on both ends.** Designate one person on the client side and one person on your side (assuming there's more than just you involved) to be the single point of contact. Get all of your feedback from that person, rather than getting bits and pieces from different people. Let them hash out their thoughts internally and gather group consensus before they talk to you so you don't have to wade through the office politics or figure out who to listen to and who to ignore. Conversely, let the client know who is in charge of receiving feedback on your end, and then that person can consolidate and share it with the rest of the team.
- **Don't take it personally.** This is hard to learn, especially for creative folks, but you are not your work and your work is not you. Criticism of your work is not a critique of you personally, so take the emotion out of it. It's just business. And who knows, the client might actually be right! Even if your client isn't following the rules above and makes the feedback about you and not the work, be gracious and respond well. If they say something offensive, you can certainly respond respectfully to that, but otherwise let it go.

An unexpected part of your job is helping clients learn how to give you the feedback you need. You may have to teach or remind them of key ideas throughout the process—but doing this is worth the effort. As you communicate expectations with clients, keep in mind the characteristics of effective feedback.

1. **Clear and specific.** Vague feedback is the worst. Statements like "I'm not feeling it," "make it pop," or "it needs more pizazz" are utterly worthless. I can change a color or a font, find a new photo, make something bigger, or move a graphic over there to make it the focus. But I can't make a design pop or "feel right" to the client unless I know more specifically what they mean by that.

2. **Timely.** In order to keep things moving and on schedule, feedback should be provided in a timely manner. The actual turnaround time will vary depending on schedules and the number of people involved, but the longer it takes to get feedback, the more momentum and focus we lose.

3. **Mindful of the overall goals.** Keeping the overall project goals in mind gives us some guardrails and helps keep us focused on what is best for the project rather than our own personal likes and dislikes. Ideally there's a compelling reason we make changes—swapping a photo with one that will engage the audience is a much better reason to change than the client not liking something for personal reasons.

4. **Given in the most appropriate format.** General feedback about overall concepts is fine for the phone, but specific edits are best given in writing. If I'm working on a printed newsletter or report, I want to get more specific design edits (move this here, resize this, etc.) and all text edits in writing—either an email or a marked up PDF is great. That way I can make the edits, and then have my proofreader go through them again to confirm that I caught them all.

5. **Candid and constructive (but not rude).** Good feedback is honest and candid—I want to know what the client really thinks so that the final product is something that solves the challenge at hand and is one they feel good about. But feedback should be constructive and respectful. It may take a few rounds of feedback to get on the same wavelength. Even if we disagree on how to arrive at the best design solution, we'll get there much faster if we play nice and work together. Also see #6.

6. **Objective.** Creative work is subjective. There are any number of reasons why I designed something the way I did and any number of reasons why someone might like or dislike it. The focus of all feedback—always—should be on the work itself not on the person. Refrain from using personal pronouns and be gracious and objective when clients

confuse you and your work. "I think this needs more whitespace" is much better than "You made everything too big and crowded." It separates the work from the person and keeps the critique on the work.

7. **Consolidated.** Feedback should be given by a single point of contact after getting consensus from the team. And ideally the team is as small as possible to keep things focused. I once worked on an annual report for a law school, and things were humming along great until the final review—my client hadn't shared the design with any of the board members on the team, and they wanted to go in a completely different direction. We were able to pivot and salvage a lot of the work we had already done, but the end result was delayed and more frantic than it should have been. I've also been in situations where I get contradicting notes from different team members, and then have to spend time figuring out who to listen to.

8. **Communicates problems, not solutions.** I want to hear what isn't working and why. The client may have thoughts on a possible solution, and I'm all ears. But I have experience and may know what will or won't work, and I want to be able to arrive at the solution on my own rather than just taking orders. If a client doesn't trust my expertise, that's a red flag.

Separate yourself from your work

Working in any creative field can be really fulfilling and rewarding. We get to create something beautiful out of nothing, and there are tens, hundreds, maybe even thousands of different ways to solve a creative problem. There's no single right answer to any given challenge—it's totally subjective. If a client doesn't like your work, it's hard not to take that personally.

Creative folks in particular put themselves in every project to some degree. The concepts you come up with, the words you write, the images you create—that all comes from somewhere deep inside of you. The technical stuff is the same for everyone, but the seeds of it come from you.

It can be hard to remove the sense of the personal from the work. But it's essential. Because at some point, the client will hate what you wrote or totally disagree with the design you sent or want your illustration to look more like that one over there. Yeah, it sucks. But you have to regroup and move on.

TAKE THE
Next Step

GOOD

☐ Whether you're giving or getting feedback, stay objective and focus on the work itself, not the people doing it.

BETTER

☐ Consolidate feedback so that it's coming from one person, in one agreed-upon format.

BEST

☐ Feedback should be specific, constructive, and focused on the overall project goal.

You don't have to *love* every project you do.

As much as we'd like to think otherwise, not every project is a portfolio piece. If you're at the top of your field and can command big budgets and lots of time and only work with clients who will say yes to whatever you want them to, you might disagree. But for everyone else, you will always have at least one project that goes in a drawer as soon as it's done.

Pesky things like budgets and deadlines mean that you only have a finite amount of time to work on something if you want to make any money on it. And clients have opinions, for better or worse, so even if you do come up with the greatest, most perfect solution that you've ever come up with and are ready to hang it on the mantle, your client might not agree.

But that's OK.

The end goal isn't to come up with the perfect design or the award-winning case study. The purpose of what we do is to solve the client's problem, do the best we can with the constraints at hand, get it done, and *move on.*

It's about solving a challenge—and it's their challenge, not yours. What you want personally doesn't matter. Yes, you should offer your advice based on your expertise, and you can push back to a certain point on a client who isn't recognizing or understanding that. But your job is to do your best work in service to their end goal.

I've worked with hundreds of clients over the years on thousands of projects. A few I'm genuinely proud of, a few I hate, and most of them I am sort of indifferent to. But most importantly, the client loved them or at least liked them well enough to approve and pay for them, which is really what I care about. The project met their goals, and so it served mine too.

TAKE THE Next Step

GOOD

☐ Remember that you are not the client and your personal preferences don't really matter.

BETTER

☐ Focus on solving a problem and making the client happy. Ideally you're proud of it too, but if not, find another aspect of it that you can celebrate and move on.

BEST

☐ Done—and paid for—is better than perfect. Aim to do the best you can within the constraints you have.

Expect the unexpected and plan ahead.

Regardless of what you do and how large that undertaking is, you know step by step how it works and what can go wrong. Your clients and customers don't. Talking about the process and possible pitfalls up front is a great idea.

My friend Teresa Torres wrote a book last year and self-published it. After signing the contract with the publishing company, she received a document outlining the scope of the project, a possible schedule, and a list a mile long of everything that could go wrong (and impact said schedule). When she told me about that, my first reaction was to be a little bit horrified. Why would you start off the working relationship with a list of what might go wrong? Why not start off on a positive note?

The more I think about it, the smarter I think that list is. Publishing a book is a huge undertaking. Someone like my friend, who is hiring that company for their first book, has no idea what is actually involved in the process. So having that list, as scary as it might have looked initially, was really helpful. It showed her exactly what the process would look like and what to realistically expect at every turn. If something went wrong on any step, she had a roadmap to know what would happen next.

I don't think that means that you need to provide a laundry list of possible issues for every project you do, but communication and honesty are vital. When I'm asked to bid on a new project, particularly one that involves lots of moving pieces, I talk about the schedule and what might impact that. I talk about what I'm going to do and what I need from the client at each step, so they understand why certain things matter. And if there's a part of the project that might get a little messy or if there's a particular issue that I've seen pop up before, I'll mention that. If the project we're working on is part of a series or will require additional tasks upon completion, it can be helpful to list out what will remain to be done next.

Even if the project itself goes off without a hitch, life happens too. My kid has a knack for getting sick when I have a huge meeting. Our power went out last November just as I was wrapping up a big deadline. A client couldn't figure out how to use his Zoom account and we spent an hour trying to get everyone set up on another platform. Plan ahead for those kinds of things too by giving yourself some buffer when you can.

Part of knowing what might go wrong is also knowing what you'll do to fix it when it does, or at least having some idea of what your contingency plan might be. Hopefully you won't need to use it, but keep your plan B in the back of your mind as you go. A good plan B is relatively easy to implement and not overly disruptive to the process. It might mean bringing on a backup web developer to take over the coding when your current contractor has an accident. It might mean having an extra proofreader available if the manuscript ends up being twice as long as you expected. It might mean switching to a different paper and an online printing vendor if the client runs late with final approval on a time-sensitive event program. Know what backup resources you might need to utilize at any given point. If it looks like that point is approaching, explain the situation to the client and make sure they know what's happening (especially if they're the reason things need to change). That way you can decide together on the best course of action. They'll appreciate that you've thought of solutions in advance.

TAKE THE Next Step

GOOD

☐ At the start of every project, think through any potential pitfalls that might arise.

BETTER

☐ Give your client an idea of the process you'll follow and mention hiccups that might pop up at particular points.

BEST

☐ Have backup plans or ideas in place in case something goes wrong. How can you, and potentially the client, work through those issues in an alternate way?

Be vigilant about copyrights.

Chances are you're reading this book because you're in a creative field, so you're likely already familiar with copyrights, and I won't say too much about them here. While it's important to pay attention to copyrights in general, it's especially important to be vigilant about them when you're the one in charge and legally on the hook for any issues.

Thankfully I don't have any big mistakes to share on this one, but I see potential issues come up all the time with my clients. In my experience, this most commonly comes up with images. Clients will do a search, and then send me a low-resolution photo that they like and ask me to use it. When that happens, I ask if they have permission to use it. Assuming I'm greeted with a blank stare, I do a reverse image search to see if I can figure out where the image came from. If it's a stock photo, we purchase it. If it's not, I'll try to convince them to let me find a stock photo for them, and I explain that if they really want this particular one, we'll need to locate the photographer and ask permission. If they really insist, which has only happened twice, then I make them put in writing that they are providing the image to me and that any copyright issues are their responsibility.

In my work with shopping malls, I'm often asked to create posters for retail tenants using photos from their websites or social media pages. I have to be really careful about who owns any images I want to use. If they're taken by the retailer, great. If they're posted by a customer, then I steer clear. No permission, no use.

I saw copyright issues around music recently. I attended a webinar where the speakers created a playlist of songs as they talked about energy and creative flow, playing clips from Spotify in the background. When the webinar recording got posted to YouTube a few days later, most of the video was silent. The speakers didn't have permission to play the songs, so they had to mute any bit of audio that included them.

AI (artificial intelligence) is another copyright minefield right now that is still being figured out, and far too expansive a subject for me to cover here. But as of this writing, anything created or modified by AI can't be copyrighted, so if you use it to write an article or create an image for a client, be aware that that content is totally up for grabs for other people to use as their own too. On top of that, AI content is sourced from existing images and text, so it's nearly impossible to know where the original content came from and whether any parts of it are copyrighted.

My advice is to only use content that you've created yourself or that you have explicit permission to use, whether it's a stock image that you paid for or a song that the composer gave you permission to use. If you're working with outside contractors, make sure the content they're giving you is OK to use too. Anything else is just asking for trouble in the form of a big, fat lawsuit with your name on it.

TAKE THE Next Step

GOOD

☐ Only use content (images, text, music, etc.) that you've created from scratch yourself.

BETTER

☐ Confirm that any provided content is copyright-free and available for you to use.

BEST

☐ Pay for stock photography and images or get explicit written permission from the owner before using any copyrighted content.

Own up to your mistakes.

Mistakes happen. Hopefully they're usually small and easy to fix (and easy to prevent in the future with a little extra care or review). But at some point, you're going to mess up on something, it's going to be big, and it'll really suck. Whether your mistake is big or small, own up to it. Don't deflect blame or throw someone else under the bus—as the boss, the buck stops with you. It is your responsibility.

Apologize and figure out how to fix the issue—to the extent that it's fixable. Offer possible solutions, and do what you can to make one happen. If there's something else you can reasonably do that takes some of the sting out of the situation, do it—like make some quick updates, send an apology, resend a file, pay to get something reprinted, discount your invoice, or offer something extra for free. Your client will be angry and may never work with you again, but at least they'll leave knowing that you did what you could to fix the situation and were professional about it. That can go a long way to maintaining your reputation.

Early in my career, I was hired to create an online calculator for social security benefits planning. The website itself was really simple and no big deal to design. Easy. The coding behind the calculator itself was really complex and required specialized development, which I obviously couldn't do, much less understand. And none of my usual contacts could do it either.

A trusted friend recommended a colleague of hers who could code what we needed. Despite the fact that he also had a full-time job, he swore he could do it in his off-time and gave me a quote. I was still green enough that I didn't know to mark up his pricing and have some financial buffer (lesson!) and wasn't too concerned about his full-time job (lesson!) and wasn't worried about not knowing him at all since he came from a friend (lesson!). I wanted the job and wanted to do it at a reasonable price, and I ignored the red flags in my gut (lesson!). We were off and running.

Things went smoothly for a few weeks, and then the coder got fed up with the long hours and the client changes, and he quit. Done with no warning. I didn't want to admit to the client that I had misjudged my team's capabilities and couldn't handle the job, so I frantically searched every job site I could find to get help. I had underestimated what the project would take, so I had no budget left over. I cycled through a few cheap developers in Romania and Belarus, but nothing worked. I finally had to come clean to the client and explain what happened and admit that I simply didn't know what to do from there. Luckily, she was understanding and had enough knowledge of the code that she was able to finish up the rest and get it launched.

What I should have done was tell her about the developer quitting the day it happened. Realistically I never should have taken on the project without having a trustworthy vendor in place, but that's another issue. Instead of being honest about what was happening and dealing with the fallout, I hid and tried to solve the problem on my own, hoping it would go well enough that she would never find out. It was exhausting. And pointless. Had I spoken up sooner, we likely could have muddled through together and gotten it finished faster.

I also would have looked a lot more professional. At the time I thought the better option was to at least appear as if I knew everything and had it handled. But the more professional thing to do would have been to speak up, admit that I was in over my head, and work to find a solution. The client appreciated my honesty when I finally did come out with it, and they might have worked with me again on something else had I done it sooner.

What if the error wasn't mine?

Regardless of who makes the mistake, be gracious and offer solutions. Everyone involved will appreciate your professionalism and ability to accept responsibility, even if the relationship ends there. If the mistake was made by someone on your team behind the scenes, then it's as if you made it. Accept responsibility, and then work with your team afterward to figure out what happened and what to do instead next time.

Clients make mistakes. You can try to minimize that by asking questions if something doesn't look quite right along the way or help keep them on track if you're not getting what you need on time. Write up a change order if their mistake causes work to be redone. At the end of the project, get official sign-off in writing so that everyone is clear that the client has reviewed everything and takes responsibility if an error pops up later on.

Vendors make mistakes too. A few years ago, I got a frantic call from a client. The event programs that had just been delivered for their annual dinner had an error—one of the main sponsor logos was blacked out. *Yikes.* The proof we had reviewed and approved had the logo right where it should be, so some sort of glitch happened during the printing process. What to do? There wasn't enough time to use the same vendor to print them again. We considered printing a sticker with the logo on it, but the time that would be needed to stick them on each brochure was prohibitive (and it wouldn't look very nice). Luckily I had another printing contact who could turn it around on a rush, so we ended up printing them again with the new vendor, and the client really appreciated that I helped them figure out what to do. Afterward, I negotiated a deal with the original printer to cut their price in half on the unusable programs, and I paid them myself. They were a trusted vendor who usually did great work, and our ongoing relationship was worth the relatively small cost to me.

Keep problems in perspective

When things go wrong, it can be hard not to get sucked into the void of feeling awful. Josh runs a web development firm and is a firm believer in staying positive. "If I could start over, one thing I would do differently is to believe that failures have something to teach us. Before setting up my business, I knew that it would not be an easy ride, but I didn't know how much a setback could affect me as a person. The time I used to waste wallowing in disappointment and self-doubt is now better spent devising a strategy for overcoming the failure."

A woman called me once in a panic on a Thursday morning. Her mother had died the night before and she wanted a keepsake program brochure designed and printed in time for the service on Sunday. Could I help her? People pleaser that I am, I said yes and dropped everything to drive an hour to her house to go over samples and talk about what she wanted. I found a printer who could rush the job. I worked all night long to design the program, got her approval, and then sent it off to print. No time for a press check—just get it done.

The programs were delivered to her on Saturday afternoon, and she was livid. The coloring on the final pieces wasn't quite right, and the text was difficult to read (though not impossible). There wasn't time to fix anything. She chewed me out for ruining her mother's funeral, and I ended up paying for the printing myself and doing the design for free.

I was gutted. And angry. I had tried to help someone, and it went spectacularly sideways. And I was paying for it all. I stewed for days.

When I look back on it now, I would put it into perspective more easily. Yes, there was a lesson or five to be learned, and it was natural to feel bad about it, but it was not worth the massive mental effort I invested in it.

Here are the main lessons I learned from the Funeral Fiasco.

1. Be really careful about doing rush projects for new people. When you're not familiar with the client, there's a lot more room for misunderstanding.
2. Be realistic about timing and bandwidth. Dropping everything and taking on a new project that required hours of driving, frantic phone calls to vendors, and staying up all night was never going to be worth it, even if I had gotten paid.
3. Clear communication is critical. I should have been clearer about what I could do and what could go wrong.

4. Make sure the client is involved in reviewing the printing proof, and always do a press check. The client either would have commented on the look and we could have fixed it, or they would have approved it and been responsible for the result.

TAKE THE Next Step

GOOD

☐ If something is amiss at any point, say something right away.
☐ When something goes wrong, remove the emotion and look critically at the situation. How big of a deal is this really?

BETTER

☐ When a mistake happens, focus on helping to find a fix rather than pointing fingers—regardless of who is at fault.

BEST

☐ When you make a mistake, speak up honestly and find a way to fix it. Find a lesson to be learned, and put processes in place to ensure that it doesn't happen again.
☐ Find at least one concrete lesson you can learn to avoid the same issue in the future.

Stand up for yourself—and get support.

You're the boss. There's no human resources or legal department to run to if an issue arises. No one in the corner office to make the hard decisions for you. It's all on you. If you're being mistreated, whether on a personal level or not getting paid or whatever the case may be, stand up for yourself. No one else can do that for you.

That can be really hard to do if you're not used to being in charge or being assertive. When something goes wrong, know who you can call for help and advice. I have a mentor, an accountant, and a lawyer who can all advise me when an issue arises. I also have a network of a few close business friends who are supportive and willing to give me advice. But ultimately the decision on what to do about it rests with me. I have to make that call—it's my business. I don't have to necessarily implement the solution myself, but I have to be the one to decide what the solution is and what the resultant action needs to be.

Sometimes that's scary and uncomfortable. But there's no way around it if you want to run your own show. Get the supports you'll need in advance and have your cheering section ready to go. Remember that this is *your* business, and you decide what happens to it. When you make brave decisions, you take responsibility for your own happiness and success, which is likely why you started running your own business in the first place.

My cheering section was a big help to me late last year. I was completely burned out, even with help, and I knew I needed to make a change by cutting some of my workload. I was miserable. My mentor asked if I knew which client or project I could cut, and I knew the answer immediately. I'd been working with this particular client for a few years and had fantasized about not having to work with her for a long time. Every project was an emergency. Emails were either sticky sweet, calling me her angel, or berated me for missing an edit or not coming up with the exact creative solution she wanted immediately. The emotional whiplash was exhausting, and I got a pit in my stomach every time their name showed up in my inbox. Why did I stick around? Money. I earned a lot of money from this client every year, and it was difficult to think about giving that up. Throw in the fact that I hate conflict, and I assumed the client and I would stay together unhappily ever after.

In one of my weekly meetups with a small group of creative business owners, I announced that I was finally going to fire this client and needed some support to keep me accountable and make it happen. They all knew the history. After the cheering stopped, we walked through some scenarios about what I should say, and they helped build my confidence—I didn't need to work with someone who treated me that way, and I would make up the money some other way. I could do this. When I got off that call, I sent my monthly invoice to the client with a note that I wouldn't be available to take any more work after the end of the month. A huge weight lifted off my shoulders as soon as I hit send, and I'm grateful for the people in my orbit that help build me up when I need it. The situation sounds a bit ridiculous now that I see it in print, but the fact is that we all need some nudging from time to time to remember how awesome we are and that we have a choice in what we do and with whom we do it.

Keep in mind that your supporters will have the best chance of giving you what you need if you're specific about what that is. Sometimes you might need advice on how to handle a situation. Sometimes you might need an accountability partner or a pep talk. And sometimes you might just need to tell someone you trust about something that went haywire with a client just to get it out of your head. Once you have what you need, remember to express your gratitude and be ready to be a cheerleader for them when it's their turn.

TAKE THE Next Step

GOOD

☐ Come up with a list of people in your life who understand what it's like to be a business owner and who are supportive and encouraging.

BETTER

☐ Be vulnerable and ask for support when you need it. Be clear on the type of support you need.

BEST

☐ Surround yourself with people who bring out the best in you and give good, solid advice that you can feel good about following. Be that person for them too.

ALMOST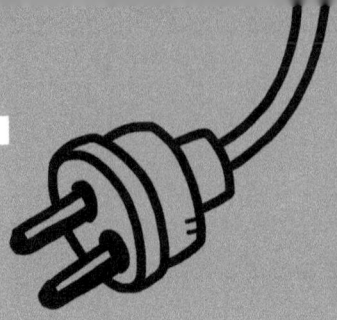
EVERYTHING WILL
WORK
AGAIN IF YOU
(UNPLUG IT)
FOR A FEW MINUTES,
INCLUDING *You.*

— ANNE LAMOTT

Hard agree. 10/10. No notes. As we explore growing your business, this wisdom is key.

NURTURE GOOD GROWTH

Work on your business continually.

Whenever you're at work, you should either be working *in* your business or *on* your business. Working *in* your business is the work you do for your clients and customers, and anything directly related to that—whatever you do that gets you paid.

Working *on* your business includes everything else that makes your business run. It's easy to put off these tasks, but doing those on-your-business tasks is what will result in the in-your-business work and help you do your work efficiently, well, and with less stress. This makes on-your-business tasks equally important—if not more so—especially when you're starting out. After a while, when you've got systems in place for a lot of your business tasks and a steady stream of clients, you will have more room to take a break—but that happens as you develop the habit of keeping a focused eye on your business.

Here are some of the things you can do to invest in your business.

- Write your next newsletter or blog. Then get a graphic for it and load it.

- Update your website. Google is a beast that needs constant feeding, so feed it with some small updates and additions to your website.
- Update your Google my business page. Feed the beast.
- Find some new prospects and reach out to them.
- Follow up with prospects and clients you haven't heard from in a while.
- Create and post something on social media. Respond to other folks you follow.
- Do your invoicing or monthly budgeting.
- Find a networking event.
- Take a class or attend a conference.
- Get up and move around for a few minutes to refocus yourself.
- Update your marketing materials.
- Create or revise your internal paperwork.
- Do your bookkeeping or taxes.
- Research contractors to get some help.
- Clean your desk.
- Read to learn something new.
- Explore an adjacent hobby.
- Order supplies.
- Volunteer. (This doesn't have to be related at all to your business, but it could end up being a low-key networking opportunity that you don't expect).
- Get outside or go for a walk to spend some time thinking and planning strategically about your business and where you want to go next.

It's easy to work on your business when business is slow. And just as easy to push it to the side when you're busy. After all, it's not paid work, right? But if you don't work *on* your business, you probably won't work *in* it very much. More than that, working on your business gives you control over it.

The dream is you just sit back and let the work come to you. Most people aren't that lucky. Jarrod started his copywriting business with the assumption that it would be easy to find clients. "I thought that people who needed my services didn't need to be sold to—they would just see my website and come to me. It was a very naive view—nothing sells without effort. However, I've learned to keep building, creating, and pivoting until there is traction. What it's all about is analyzing your traffic and your audience to see what they want and what they find the most valuable. And then, pivoting, updating, and creating your services and products to match those trends."

I had a lot of luck in my early days. When I started out, I responded to an ad on Craigslist and got a monthly retainer with a design firm in San Francisco—they were amazing and taught me a lot, all while giving me steady monthly income. Then I got hired to do some work by a former client at my previous job, and then she referred me to someone else, and it snowballed from there. I was always really busy and didn't have to market myself, other than doing the work and being the kind of designer that was worth keeping.

But over time, I realized being lucky wasn't getting me everything I wanted. As someone reliant on referrals and repeat business, I was completely at the mercy of all of those clients—they decided what I could work on, how much I could charge for it, and when it had to be done. Had they gone away, I would have had nothing left, and no systems in place to replace them. Without going after the prospects I wanted, there was zero chance that I'd be able to grow on my terms or shape my business into what I wanted it to be.

I recognized that I needed to market myself, but I never made time for it. I was so busy with client work. I thought I would focus on marketing later. It wasn't until the fall of 2019 that I finally took control and started my newsletter. I finally realized if I wanted to potentially go after new clients and grow my business, I was going to need to be more visible more often.

My first newsletter was a simple "Happy Thanksgiving" message with a note that I was starting up a newsletter—super easy to write and send. The next month, I again sent a very simple "Happy Holidays" email with my holiday office closure—easy and painless. I really got in the groove three months later when the world shut down, and the letter I wrote about it resonated with a lot of my clients. I discovered that people were connecting with what I was putting out into the world, and more importantly, I discovered that I *love* writing and could suddenly see content topics everywhere I looked. Marketing is work, but it isn't all drudgery. Once I got a handle on that, I started doing monthly email outreach and being more active on LinkedIn.

That's really all I do. I keep it simple and do what is manageable for me. Everybody's life and business needs are different. Rather than focusing on the ROI (return on investment), what matters is that I'm going after what I want, being proactive instead of reactive. If my biggest client goes away tomorrow, I'll just ramp up the marketing I'm doing now, and I don't have to start from scratch. When business is good, I have the freedom to try different things when the stakes are low.

Once you're clear on the things you need and want to do every month to work on your business, carve out the time for it. I do the bulk of my invoicing once a month, so I block off a few hours in the evening on the last day of the month to get them all done and an hour the following morning to send them out. I know I need an hour or two on the first day of the month to prep my financial paperwork for my bookkeeper. No matter how busy I am, that time is blocked off.

My newsletter goes out once a month, usually near a holiday if there is one. So I know I need to plan ahead and get my letter written in time for my copywriter to make edits, and then block off time to create the graphics, load it in Mailchimp, and send it off. The same thing goes for my new LinkedIn newsletter, sent once a month. I send a few outreach emails to prospective clients weekly, so I need to carve out an hour for that too.

If you're having trouble making it a priority, ask yourself what it will take for you to do it. Do you need an accountability partner? Do you need to get up early and do it before your workday starts? Do you need to find or start a group of like-minded folks who are doing the same task and meet once a week? Or all of the above (like me). Be honest with yourself and know what it will take for you to get it done.

TAKE THE Next Step

GOOD

☐ Add a list of the business items that you need to complete to your weekly task list and work on them as you find time.

BETTER

☐ Set aside some time every week to work on your business and block it off on your calendar.

BEST

☐ Know yourself. If you need support or accountability to get work done on your business, find the partners you need and schedule it. Make your own work a priority.

Get real—having it all does not exist.

This topic is a bit of a downer, but having realistic expectations for yourself and your career are key to success.

As your business grows, you'll have more choices to make about how to spend your time and honor what's important to you. The trick is to figure out what you have to say yes to, what you can delegate or get help with, and what you can let go—and then live with it. So maybe you hire a virtual assistant, ask a neighbor to tutor the kids, and order some takeout.

Part of my reason for going out on my own was that I thought it would give me more flexibility over my schedule when I eventually had kids. The flexibility is real. I had visions of sitting at my desk, sunlight streaming through the window, creative juices flowing, deadlines being met, while my baby napped peacefully nearby. On that front, I was completely and totally delusional.

By the time my son was born, I'd been in business for myself for ten years. I was used to working long days and late nights, and assumed I'd be able to juggle a baby too. After all, babies sleep a lot, right? I found out fast that kids don't usually do what you expect or want them to.

My son rarely slept. He certainly didn't care about my deadlines or how tired I was or that I had a meeting. We enrolled him in full-time daycare after three months, which was the only way I was able to get any work done. But he had a knack for getting sick precisely forty-five minutes before every meeting. So we needed a backup plan. Sometimes that meant that my husband had to leave work and come home, sometimes we went to Grandma's, and sometimes I had to switch to a phone call at the last minute.

Things got a little better once my son started kindergarten, and then eight months later the pandemic hit. Suddenly I was sharing an office and found myself constantly interrupted by iPhone alarms, Zoom classes, schoolwork questions, and requests for snacks and things to do. Add that to a very full workload (no time for sourdough starters here!), and I felt like I was being pulled in a million different directions and failing at all of them. When I was working, I felt like I wasn't being a great mother or wife. And when I was mothering and wifing, I felt like I should be taking care of another deadline or working on a project that I really wanted to do.

Over time we got into a more manageable groove, but it was still hard. The sentences I uttered most in a day were often "I'm sorry, honey, I can't—I'm working" or "Just a minute, please," both of which feel lousy to have to say over and over again. Several of the rooms in my house were littered with Legos and craft kits, but that was OK for the time—it meant that my son was occupying himself with his "creations," which bought me some peace and quiet. It got cleaned up eventually.

No, this is not a glowing success story. My house is covered in dog hair and dirty socks, and my office is full of PTA supplies. I will never have a photo-ready home or feel like I've got all of my shit together, but that's OK. The important stuff gets done and everyone in the house is loved and taken care of, so the rest really doesn't matter in the end. My life is a work in progress and yours will be too. But keep evaluating your goals and how you spend your time. As an entrepreneur, you have more freedom than most to make your life how you want it to be.

Own your goals and your dreams, and be realistic about the tradeoffs you need to make to realize them. You can't do everything or be everything. Know your strengths and your limits and make peace with what you cannot do. We all make choices about what to say yes and no to. The key is to be aware of our choices and make sure they align with the life we want to live.

TAKE THE *Next Step*

GOOD

☐ Each day, look at your obligations and decide what must be done versus what can be done. Focus on the must-dos and fill in any spaces with the can-dos.

BETTER

☐ Do what you can, and give yourself some grace on the rest.

BEST

☐ Delegate whatever tasks you can afford and focus on the to-dos that matter most to you. Let everything else go.

NOTES

Foster creativity instead of forcing it.

There will be times when you've got a deadline coming up and you aren't feeling inspired or just don't feel like working. But deadlines (and clients) don't care whether you're in the mood—shit's gotta get done.

Creativity can't be forced—and I'm not just talking about graphic design or painting or anything else art-related. Working through any type of challenge or task that requires focused thinking isn't always easy and takes the time it takes, especially if you're not feeling it. There are things you can try to get yourself in the mood and get your creative juices flowing.

1. **Take a break.** Run a quick errand, call a friend, watch an episode of your favorite show, or read a book. Doesn't matter what you do during the break, just get away from the computer or notebook or easel and go somewhere else. Taking a shower almost always works for me. It's a brief task that I can commit to for a short period of time, is something I need to do anyway, feels good, and forces me to focus on something else. Sometimes the idea I need pops into my head as soon as the water hits me; other times it just gives me a little break and a bit of a reset, which is helpful too.

2. **Take a nap.** This only works if you're at home, but maybe a short power nap is what you need to give your thinking cap a rest and your body a bit of energy. I almost always get some of my best ideas as soon as I quiet down and try to sleep, almost as if my subconscious has been waiting for the rest of my inner voices to shut up for a bit. Even if you don't end up sleeping, sitting quietly and letting your mind wander can do the trick.

3. **Get outside.** Take a walk around the block and get some fresh air. Smell some flowers. Lay in the grass or sit in the hot tub. The space around you might spark something creative. Get out of your head and into your body.

4. **Do some research.** Whenever I'm stuck, a search for whatever type of project I'm working on is one of the first things I do. I also like to peruse things like stock illustration websites, magazines, and Instagram to see what other people are doing in general that might spark an idea for me. I have colleagues who watch specific types of cartoons or go to museums.

And when all else fails? Just get started. Commit to fifteen to thirty minutes and just get something down on screen or paper. If you're still struggling after that and have time before the deadline, take another break and try again later. But you'll more likely find that getting started is the hardest part. Once you have a little momentum, it's a lot easier to keep going, even if it's a slog and you're just doing it to get it done.

TAKE THE
Next Step

GOOD

☐ Think about what energizes and inspires you, and find quick ways to do that when you aren't feeling motivated.

BETTER

☐ Take a break and focus on something else for a bit that will get you out of your head and into your body.

BEST

☐ Commit to working on the task for fifteen minutes and just do something. Chances are, you'll get in a groove and stick around for more than fifteen minutes.

Automate and templatize what you can.

Over time, you'll find that there are certain tasks that you need to do over and over again. Projects need estimates. Prospects need proposals or samples. New clients need a contract. Customers want to see a newsletter. If you're creating each of these types of items from scratch every time, stop it.

Whenever you can, create a template so that all you have to do is open it up, swap out the relevant info, and send it off. Especially when it comes to proposals and sample packets, you're not getting paid yet, so you want to do as little work as possible but still present your best self. A good template will allow you to do that. Just be sure you proofread it and then proofread it again to make sure none of the old contact info is in there before you send it to the new person.

If there are things you can automate, like sending estimates or contracts, signing people up for your newsletter, and scheduling meetings with clients, do it. If you're thinking that's impersonal, it's not. Automating these tasks allows you to be present for the interactions that matter most.

Last year I signed up for Calendly, an online scheduling service that connects to my calendar and lets clients schedule meetings with me at whatever time I have available. When someone wants to meet with me, I send them my link, and they can select the date, time, and method that works for them. I also signed up for HelloSign, and now it's easy for clients to sign contracts and estimates with a single mouse click. The recipients appreciate being able to sign or pick a date and time with the touch of a button rather than emailing back and forth. And it's easier for me too.

Social media is pretty easy to automate these days, too, with some up-front effort. I have a colleague who created a suite of social media images using one template, created a handful of images for each of the blog posts she'd written by just updating the text on the image, and loaded them all into SocialBee. Now she has two years of social media posts ready to go without needing to lift a finger. I know other colleagues who use similar services to schedule their own campaigns.

TAKE THE
Next Step

GOOD

☐ Make a list of the documents you use the most, and turn them into templates that are easy to duplicate and update.

BETTER

☐ Find business tasks like scheduling meetings that you can automate through a service.

BEST

☐ Hire a virtual assistant or delegate the updating of your business paperwork or other graphics so that you only have to do a quick review each time. Let someone else take care of the rest.

Work alone without having to *be* alone.

I work in a home office alone, and I always have (at least when there hasn't been a pandemic classroom in the corner). But I don't feel alone. There were times early in my solo career where I did feel lonely, but I had enough family, friends, and hobbies to fill in the spaces when I wasn't working.

As I got busier and had to spend more time at my desk, there were a few years where I did feel pretty isolated and like I was stuck in my own little bubble. Over time, I've found lots of ways to connect with other folks so that I never felt lonely—sometimes I even feel like I'm getting too much connection and need to scale back.

These are the ways I connect with other like-minded work friends.

Business and trade organizations.

When I started working for myself, I thought it would be a good idea to join the local chamber of commerce and attend meetings. That's what business owners do, right? Yes and no. The group wasn't a good fit for me—my non-profit target market wasn't hanging out there—but I did meet a new friend there who introduced me to a different networking group that was a better fit. Other trade organizations might have meetings that you can attend, and I know other solopreneurs who love groups like BNI (Business Network International) and Toastmasters. There are lots of options!

Networking groups.

The idea of traditional networking makes me feel a little ill—so many smarmy salespeople pushing stuff I don't need or want. I've been lucky enough to find a few networking groups over the years that preach connection and generosity versus sales, and those groups are wonderful. I don't necessarily meet clients there, which isn't really my goal anyway. I meet other business owners who are dealing with the same issues I am. Suddenly I have people to vent to or ask questions to, and they understand. I'm currently in two different groups: one exclusively for consultants in the Pacific Northwest who work with nonprofits and one for folks in creative fields. The groups are great places to learn from other business owners, and they provide me with a great referral network.

Business coaching groups.

I've worked with a few coaches in the past, with varying levels of success (whatever that means). One of my favorites was a coach who worked with small, women-owned businesses, and I met a great group of women there—one of whom I'm still friends with ten years later.

Coworking spaces (real or virtual).

I had a membership at a swanky business club for a while, which wasn't a good fit for a number of reasons, but it gave me a place to go to be around other people and get work done in a different setting. I have colleagues who rent space in small coworking offices with other folks, and there are other spaces you can rent for the hour or the day if you want a change of scenery for a while. During the pandemic, virtual coworking became a big thing in my circles, and I *love* it. I check in with a group on Zoom at the appointed time, tell them what I plan to work on, and then turn off my camera for an hour or two before checking in again at the end. There's something comforting about knowing that other people are working *with* me. I love having the accountability and being able to connect with other people without having to leave my house. Don't have a group of people to cowork with? Use a service like Focusmate (focusmate.com)—with options for different time intervals and locations, you can almost always find someone somewhere to work with.

My mentor.

I've been working with my mentor Ilise off and on for over ten years, and it has been one of the best things I've done. Not only do I get great advice from her and regular contact with someone who isn't one of my clients, but her network has become my network—it's an amazing community of folks that I don't know what I'd do without. Mentors come in lots of formats—maybe it's someone you worked with at a previous company, someone you met through a business contact, or a coach that you hire. If you know people who have mentors, ask how they found them and try a few out.

Accountability groups.

I am great at getting deadlines done for other people, but I'm lousy at doing them for myself. So accountability groups are a big help for me. Sometimes it's as simple as emailing a colleague to tell them that I'm committing to work on x for the next hour, and then checking in when I'm done. I am currently signed up for two weekly groups: one that forces me to carve out an hour each week to work on new client outreach and one that forces me to carve out two hours for writing (the result of which you're reading right now).

Work at a coffee shop.

I occasionally meet up with a colleague at a local coffee shop—we bring our laptops and work together separately for a few hours. I don't like to do this on my own as I find it hard to focus, but a small café could be a great place for you to sit with a treat and get some work done.

Buddy retreats.

You're self-employed, so if you really want to go big, create your own retreat. My friend Anita (a finance consultant) and I have done our own end-of-year business retreat. We get a room for two nights at a nice hotel and carve out time to work on our own business goals for the year, peppered with spa treatments and lively discussions over fancy meals in between. It's so much fun and so productive! This only works if you're with someone who is also serious about getting work done during the working part of the retreat though.

Social media groups.

Social media can be a little tricky since it's all online, but they can be great places to meet like-minded folks and get advice. Facebook groups like Freelancing Females and Millo Mastermind have been helpful to me in finding contractors to work with or getting advice on how other business owners would handle a specific client issue. And there's almost always someone online, so if you're feeling lonely, you can reach out and someone will most likely be there.

Whatever you try, show up with genuine curiosity and a spirit of generosity. You never know who you'll meet or who they know or where the connection will lead.

TAKE THE
Next Step

GOOD

☐ Try out a coworking space or attend a networking event and get to know the people in your area.

BETTER

☐ Join a networking group or trade organizations in your particular area of interest, especially those geared towards freelancers and entrepreneurs.

BEST

☐ Test out some small accountability groups and coworking sessions until you find your people.

Be a good referral partner.

Referrals are the lifeblood of any thriving business. I wouldn't be where I am today without clients telling their friends and colleagues about me and other freelance partners bringing me on to their projects or sending me prospects that aren't a good fit for them.

Testing out and vetting new vendors can be difficult and time-consuming, and working with new people is always a bit of a crapshoot. A good referral has already been tested by someone else and is more likely to be a good fit. Referrals won't magically fall into your lap without some effort on your part. What does it mean to be a good referral partner?

1. **Make sure you're worth referring.** Anyone who recommends you is putting their own reputation on the line too, so make it worth their effort by doing good work, giving good customer service, and generally behaving in the way that puts your best foot forward. If a client refers you and you do a lousy job, they aren't likely to recommend you again.

2. **Tell people how they can best refer you.** Ensure that clients and colleagues know that you welcome referrals, who your ideal client is, and what type of work you most want to do. That way you're top of mind when those types of prospects or projects come along. Conversely, if there are types of work that you don't want to do or industries you don't want to work with, giving people a heads up in advance saves their time (and yours).

3. **Look for potential partnerships that benefit all involved.** Web developers and graphic designers are a match made in heaven, as are designers and copywriters. Find creative people who do what you don't do, and partner together to expand your service offerings. Now you've got someone else you trust trying to find potential work for you too!

4. **Create a referral agreement with colleagues.** I have an informal agreement with one of my usual web developers—any time I refer her for a website project that doesn't involve design or isn't a good fit for me for some reason, she gives me a 5 percent finders fee when she successfully wins the bid. And vice versa. We don't have it written down anywhere—some people choose to do that and make it an official contract—but our handshake agreement works for both of us. Incentivizing partners with some sort of monetary reward makes both of us more likely to refer clients to each other rather than referring to someone else. You can also offer clients a discount on a future project for every referral they provide.

5. **Show gratitude.** When someone refers you, show your appreciation. That could be as simple as saying thank you or might mean sending a gift. A former client recommended me for a big project, and when I won the bid I sent her an expensive bottle of champagne and some chocolates. People appreciate the acknowledgment that they've done something good for you. And saying thank you also makes it more likely that they'll refer you again in the future.

TAKE THE Next Step

GOOD

☐ Do your best work and be professional, and don't be afraid to let happy clients know that you're open to referrals.

BETTER

☐ Refer your colleagues for projects, when appropriate, and let them know what types of projects are the best fit for you too.

BEST

☐ Partner with other freelancers who offer services that are complementary to yours (like a graphic designer and a printer or a copywriter and a proofreader). Look for projects that you can do together.

Stop being a bottleneck—delegate!

When it comes to designing stuff for other people, meeting external deadlines, or helping someone else get something done, I'm a whiz. When it comes to doing my own projects, the opposite tends to be true. I know if I'm holding something up for any period of time, it's time to hand it off to someone else.

Running a business takes a lot of work and requires the wearing of a lot of different hats. Take some of them off! If I don't have time to figure out all of the stuff I don't know or my indecision is slowing me down, then it's a much better use of my time and money to pay someone who can get it done for me while I'm doing billable work.

As a graphic designer, I felt a ton of pressure to design an amazing website myself. But I had two things working against me—I was constantly swamped with client work and totally paralyzed by indecision when it came to figuring out what I wanted for the look of the site. After months of delay, I finally realized that it wasn't going to happen if I didn't pass it off, and I hired a trusted colleague to design and build it for me. She helped give me a concrete list of tasks to complete (copywriting, pulling portfolio images, etc.) and then made it happen. And I love it. If I hadn't hired her, I'd probably still have my old site up or some sort of eternal "coming soon" page.

Even now that I have a really strong brand presence and a general style that makes it easier for me to design my stuff, I still get stuck sometimes. Earlier this year I hired one of my usual contract designers to refresh my proposal template for me. She gave me a fresh set of eyes on it, and I was able to get out of the way and actually get it done.

In order to save mental space, time, and frustration, here are some of the hats I don't wear any more, at least not very often or not by myself.

- **Proofreading.** I do a lot of little social media event graphics and was having trouble keeping up with all of the reviewing (and frankly not doing as great a job as I should have because I needed to move so fast). So I hired a proofreader, and it was game-changing. Now when my team builds suites of graphics for multiple events, they get loaded to Dropbox and reviewed by someone who is taking her time. All I have to do is send them off.
- **Copywriting.** I do all of my writing, including newsletters, blog posts, and the words you're reading here, but I have a trusted copywriter who reviews it all and makes suggestions to take it to the next level. She also does the bulk of the copywriting for my clients.

- **Website updates.** I know enough WordPress to get myself into trouble. I can make basic updates to my blog and portfolio, but I send everything else to my developer and she keeps me updated and running securely.
- **Bookkeeping/financial advising/accounting.** I have a bookkeeper who enters everything into QuickBooks for me every month and follows up with delinquent accounts, a financial advisor who helps me invest the money I make, and an accountant who makes sure it all comes together at the end of the year. The peace of mind I have knowing that I don't have to worry about the rules is invaluable.
- **Production work.** I have a network of contractors of all stripes that I hire to handle production work. My time is better spent on the initial high-level design work and working on my business rather than versioning out a poster into fifteen smaller graphics or formatting a one hundred-page book into an existing template. I still review and refine things, but the grunt work is handled elsewhere.
- **Research.** Occasionally I need to do some research on a potential client or new software or to gather information for an outreach campaign, and I have someone I can call for that.

Some of the hats I haven't yet taken off that you might: social media, newsletters, proposals/estimates, shipping and mailing, project management, and invoicing. If there's something you need to get done but you consistently find that you aren't doing it or you just plain don't want to, it's worth it to get out of the way and hire someone else. Especially if it's a task that will get you paid or frees you up to work on something else and make money in the meantime.

Hiring help in five easy steps

Delegating work and bringing on contract help can feel scary the first time you do it, but it doesn't have to be. Once you know what kind of help you need, the basic steps are pretty easy. Finding the actual right fit for you will (hopefully) be the hardest part.

Outsourcing certain tasks like bookkeeping or accounting are generally pretty simple and covered earlier in the book. But let's assume here that you need more creative help and that you're looking for a freelancer. Whenever I find myself needing to hand off design work to someone new, here's how I do it.

1. I have a pretty robust network of creative folks, so I start by asking around there. Has my mentor talked to any designers lately who need more work? Who are my colleagues using that they really like? Once that network is tapped, I head to Facebook and LinkedIn and look at

some of the freelance design groups I belong to. I look at the posts to see what designers are looking for work, check out their portfolios, and then email them. If I'm not getting what I need there, I'll head to Upwork, post a job, and try someone new.

2. Once I've found someone that I think might be a good fit, I interview them. Depending on how I found them, that might be a really quick and simple conversation. I lay out my needs, budget, timeline, and expectations. If the freelancer is in alignment with me and we have a good personality fit, then we move to the next step. If it's someone new, it's a more in-depth process to make sure their experience and skills match what I need.

3. I write up a quick contract outlining our engagement. I generally like to hire contractors on an ongoing basis, so the contract usually is a simple letter stating what their hourly rate is, how many hours per week or month we'll work together (if that's known, otherwise I leave that off and just say that it's on an as-needed basis), what sorts of tasks we'll do together, how often they'll bill me, and when they can expect to be paid. I also make it clear that they're a contractor and not an employee, and that our agreement is in effect until it needs to be changed (usually when they increase their hourly rate) or terminated (ideally with a few weeks' notice). I also send them a blank W-9 form to fill out and return to me.

4. I test them out to see if we're really a good fit. If I don't know them at all, I'll start with smaller projects that have less at stake and then build from there. Creative talent can be difficult to judge from a portfolio—you never really know if the work is fully theirs or how much art direction or editing went on to get the final product. Sometimes I think a designer will have a style that works for my clients and that isn't the case. Starting small lets me get a sense of their creative and working styles without investing too much time or money.

5. If things are going well, we continue. If I'm not loving the work or the relationship, we move on. If I pay them over $600 in a calendar year (and if they're not incorporated), I use their signed W-9 to issue a 1099 tax form in January. The form is easy to fill out, using services like Track1099 or QuickBooks.

There aren't enough hours in the day for you to do all of the things, even if that's all you do, so delegation is the only way. Stephanie Scheller, founder and chief event designer for Grow Disrupt, agrees. "For some reason, I thought I could build and scale a multimillion-dollar business alone. I've learned that that's crazy! The more people I bring on, carefully and selectively, the more I'm able to accomplish because I can lean into my energy advantage and doing the things I *love*. The business grows faster the more I lean out of the day-to-day and into leadership!"

TAKE THE
Next Step

GOOD

☐ Make a list of all of the hats you wear as a business owner. Pick one that you would love to delegate and research options.

BETTER

☐ When you're stuck on a task and holding up progress elsewhere, delegate that task.

BEST

☐ Delegate all tasks that need to be done but don't need to be done by you (or that you don't want to do).

Have a backup plan.

No, not a backup plan as in "what are you going to do if this entrepreneur thing doesn't work out." A backup plan as in "I'm flooded with work or I want to go on vacation—I need some backup."

Your need for help might be short—just a day or two. Maybe you'll get food poisoning two days before a big deadline that can't be moved. Maybe you'll have a family emergency and need someone else to be your main point of contact so you can be offline. Maybe you've got a big client fire to put out and other things are piling up in the meantime. Figure out who can help you in a pinch and have a conversation in advance.

Eventually, you're going to want to take some extended time off. Maybe you'll go on a three-week cruise in Europe. Maybe you'll have a baby, or a surgical procedure that requires some recovery. Or maybe you just need a break but don't want to totally close your business while you're doing it. Anything is possible with a little advance planning. Figure out who you know and trust to run things in your absence and set the ground rules for what they will and won't do. Decide how available you'll be in terms of answering questions or giving direction. Then let all of your clients know well in advance and make introductions before you go.

In April we had a wedding to attend during my son's spring break, so we decided to tack on a week at the beach and take a real vacation. I knew that I really didn't want to have to work during that time, especially with some of the travel that would be required. About a month before I left, I started warning my clients that I was going to be away so that we could make sure we scheduled around it. I also reached out to a colleague of mine that I trust to see if she was available that week and willing to step in if needed—I've known her for years and she has also done work for me before. We wrapped up what needed to be finished and pushed out the projects that could wait. My colleague stepped in to take on some work while I was away, and it was a win for everyone.

Don't let anxiety keep you from getting away

It's hard to leave, but the flexibility to get away is likely one of the reasons you started your own business in the first place. Don't miss out on the benefits of your hard work. Here are some of the questions that make me anxious about leaving—and the truth that lets me be free to take care of myself.

- **What if something goes wrong while I'm out and I'm not around to fix it?** Big deal. It'll be there to fix when you get back. If you're working on something that's really critical and genuinely important, then give your client a way to contact you in an emergency. Or better yet, have someone you trust standing by to help in your absence. If they call, you can decide whether to deal with it then or tell them how they can fix it themselves. You get to decide what issues are urgent enough to demand your time.
- **What if my client works with someone else while I'm gone and likes them better than me?** So what? That could happen even when you aren't on vacation. So take the break. You'll be refreshed for your next opportunity.
- **What if my dream client reaches out to me and I'm not there to talk to them?** They can wait. This actually happens to me all the time. Every time I plan a vacation for more than a day or two, I get a call from a new client. Every time. Maybe I should plan vacations more often, right? Even when people are excited to get started, they're almost always willing to wait. And if they can't or won't wait, then they're not the right fit for me right now.
- **What if my clients have projects for me and I need the work?** It's all about scheduling. Talk to your clients in advance. Let them know when you'll be out and what they can expect. Plan for it, and then everyone gets what they need. If your clients really need help now or if you're in the middle of something that needs to keep moving while you're away, then find someone to help you. Bring in a colleague that you trust, and they can take over while you take a swim.
- **But my clients really need this work done! By me! Right now!** Stop it. It's like the flight attendant says: you need to put your own oxygen mask on first or you'll be completely useless and unable to help anybody else. They likely say it more nicely, but it's true. If you're exhausted and likely resentful, you're not doing your best work. If your body doesn't tell you that you're done, your clients might. So close up the laptop, shut down the phone, and don't feel guilty about it for a second.

TAKE THE
Next Step

☑ ☑

GOOD

☐ If you don't have people you trust who can help you when you need it, reach out to your network and ask who other people use.

BETTER

☐ Try out some of your referred resources on projects in advance of your departure or before you have an emergency. Give them limited responsibility while you're away (like have them working but not interacting with clients).

BEST

☐ Alert your clients, choose a trusted replacement, and hand over the reins with confidence.

NOTES

Take good care of yourself.

You are valuable. You are your business's biggest asset. Likely one of the reasons you chose this career path was so you could *enjoy your life*. So, please, even though this path isn't easy, don't be miserable. Make sure to enjoy the fruits of your labor.

Exploit your flexibility

My favorite thing about being self-employed? Flexibility. With a laptop and a cell phone, I can work from just about anywhere at any time. As long as I meet my deadlines, it doesn't matter if I'm at my desk or in a lounge chair—and no one has to be the wiser. In fact, the words you're reading right now were written on a lovely California summer day, sitting poolside in the shade while my son takes a swim.

In the past, I've worked everywhere from a beach house in Kauai to a cabin on a river in Leavenworth, Washington, to a swanky hotel in Warsaw, Poland. I admit that some of those work sessions were done during vacations when I should have been relaxing, but the fact is that I am able to get stuff done all over the world. Most of the time I don't even need to tell anyone that I'm not at my home office.

Even on a smaller scale, I can control my own schedule. If I want to sleep in or shut down early, no one can tell me I can't. If I want to take a long lunch with a friend or take a walk in the morning or just play hooky for a few hours or a day, I can. If I want to block off Fridays for personal projects or not accept client meetings on Mondays, the only person stopping me is me! It involves a little planning to make sure I get all of my deadlines met, but otherwise I don't have to answer to anyone or feel guilty that I'm not working. As long as my clients know what to expect from me on their projects and when I'll communicate, they don't need to know where I am or what I'm doing otherwise. An easy way I do that is to simply say "I'll plan get this back to you by [date]. Will that work?" or "Can I get this back to you on Friday?" The client knows when to expect that project from me, and as long as I meet that target, it doesn't matter what I'm doing in between now and then.

I have admittedly been pretty lousy at taking advantage of this freedom in the past, but I'm doing it more and more these days.

Ruth is a social media marketer who does this too. "I started freelancing to get more control over my work and personal life. I wanted to be available to my kids when they had field trips or special events at school. I wanted to enjoy more time with friends and family when the opportunities arose, even if it was in the middle of a normal workday. It took me years to get to that point where I could care more about my time than my income. I've finally reached that point though, because I have built a highly successful, repeatable, predictable business that makes work feel less like work."

What do you want to do with your flexibility? What dreams did you have about life as an entrepreneur before you started your business? What are the most important values in your life right now? Now make it happen.

Take real vacations

You can't work 24/7. Even if you want to or feel like you have to. It's not sustainable. Breaks are essential for rest and recharging, both mentally and physically. Depending on what you do during your break, you might even get inspired and be more productive and creative when you get back to work.

For years I thought that I was so indispensable to my clients that I couldn't possibly take time off. Or if I wasn't indispensable, they'd find someone else during my absence and never work with me again. Neither of which was true.

Remember you have to actually shut down for it to be a break. Set your out-of-office message, change your voicemail greeting, and keep the laptop closed. Otherwise, you're just working remotely from a more scenic office. If your family or friends are there too, you'll feel resentful that you have to work, and they'll be annoyed that you're not spending time with them. And that's a shitty way to spend a vacation. I know, because I have done that on almost every vacation I've taken in the last twenty years. I've been stuck at the computer with slow Wi-Fi and mounting frustration while my family went on a hike, working late nights or early mornings while everyone else slept in. And whose fault was that? *Mine.* Nobody made me give up my free time—I did that all on my own.

Vacations don't have to be long or expensive to be valuable. A two-week trip to Hawaii isn't necessarily better than a weekend at a local campsite. If you love sleeping in a bag in the woods and are going to feel more relaxed and ready to go after a day or two of that, then do it! If that's going to make you miserable, then come to the beach with me—I'll meet you in the spa.

Everyone needs a break now and then, and the world won't end if you go offline.

Treat self-care like medical care

This one is so important that I'll say it again louder: SELF-CARE IS HEALTH CARE! Doesn't matter whether it's your physical health or your mental health—taking care of it matters, often in ways you don't realize until it's too late. It took me *years* to fully get this, and I wonder sometimes how different my life would be if I'd gotten it sooner.

For the first few years of my business, I worked constantly. I played ice hockey a few nights a week and saw my chiropractor a few times a month, but other than that I worked. I regularly pulled all-nighters, sometimes three times a week, and I alternated between coffee or Diet Coke to stay awake and sleeping pills to make myself fall asleep when I had the chance. I was single and lived alone, so if I wasn't out with friends, I was at my desk.

Not only was I perpetually exhausted, but I worked so much that at one point I gave myself a serious case of carpal tunnel in my right hand. Luckily for me, one of my clients was a medical doctor who specialized in ergonomics and pain management, so I went to see him and got a cortisone shot in my wrist. That shot was serious enough to make me realize that I couldn't keep working at the same pace if I wanted to keep the use of my hands (and who doesn't?). I got help with work, wore wrist braces, and learned to recognize the signs so I could stop it sooner next time. These days when I start to feel a little click in my wrist after a long week of work, I know it's time to brace up and shut down.

Even though I was playing hockey, any health benefits I got from that were drowned out (literally) by beer with my teammates or the junk I was eating at home. I felt awful physically. At some point during that time I managed to leave my desk long enough to meet my husband, and he is an amazing cook. But I was still working too much, not eating as well as I should, and not sleeping. I was completely and utterly miserable.

With the help of the occasional emergency spa weekend (our agreed-upon alternative to a seventy-two-hour hold), and a three-week honeymoon vacation followed by a honeymoon pregnancy, I was able to slow down just a bit. Once my son was born, I was too tired to keep up the same pace and finally started getting some real help.

One of the best things I did? Go to the doctor and talk about my fatigue. Turns out I had major sleep apnea and had been suffocating in my sleep, every night, for *years*. That one single thing is something I really regret. I wonder how many years of life I may have lost by thinking I was too busy to take an hour to go see a doctor.

Meera Watts, owner of Siddhi Yoga International, learned this the hard way too. "I've always been the type of person who would push herself to the point where her body used to cry for help. I used to work all hours of the day and night when I first started my business in order to attain my goals. This resulted in a constant state of exhaustion and frustration, creating issues in my personal life as well. For the sake of my dreams, I used to put my mental and physical health on the back burner. Looking back, I believe it is critical to give your body the rest it requires in order to function effectively. Now I try to prioritize both my work and my health at the same time."

Julie is a woodworker who takes her mental health more seriously now too. "So much of the early years of building my business was sleepless nights followed by days full of anxiety. Of course, if I knew I was going to make it, it would have been a little easier to not drive myself crazy! Maintaining one's mental health is one of the hardest parts of being a small business owner and operator, and I wish I had taken that part more seriously. I wish I could go back and give more attention to my family and my partner and my friends, because being all-consumed by your work can really start to wear on you and those around you."

Don't take as long as I did to learn these lessons. Don't wait. Here are a few of the activities I now do to help keep myself going.

- **Massage.** I joined a massage club about a mile from my house, and the membership fees allow me to get one massage a month at a discounted rate. Paying for it in advance forces me to go, and I'm always grateful that I do. It's a lot easier to function when my shoulders aren't on fire, and when I feel like I can have an hour to myself doing something that feels good.
- **Chiropractic.** I've been going to a chiropractor since I was sixteen to deal with migraine headaches. I feel so much better after I go that I've continued to do maintenance on and off ever since.
- **Sleep.** I make it a point to go to bed on time and aim for seven to eight hours every night. That doesn't mean that I always make that happen and don't occasionally work late, but as I get older I just physically can't function without adequate sleep. I don't miss being at my desk at 4 a.m., watching the sun come up, deciding whether to sleep for a few hours or power through the day.
- **Hiring help.** I used to focus on the "money going out" aspect of hiring help, but I'm getting so much more in return. I'm getting a lift knowing that I don't have to do it all myself. If I'm working on another project at the same time, I'm getting twice as much done and making more money and getting some free time back. Assuming the help you're hiring is good, trustworthy, and reliable, it's totally worth the money.
- **Therapy.** Whether it's through an actual therapist, my mentor, or good friends, talking through what's going on is hugely helpful. That doesn't mean that I unload on everyone I talk to, but I know who I can call for some advice or just a patient ear.
- **Exercise.** Between my workload and motherhood, I gained a lot of weight. I was sitting all the time, eating too much, and very rarely getting up and moving around. The idea of taking an hour to walk or go

to a gym seemed out of reach. My solution? I got a standing desk and a walking treadmill, and that made a huge difference for me. When I'm in a groove, I can walk for about two hours over the course of a day and still get my work done. It's not the same as going outside, but still gets me moving a bit.

- **Breaks.** I'm trying to be more conscious about taking breaks, even if it's just stepping away for ten minutes to take a deep breath outside while I get the mail. Taking extended time off still feels difficult to me, but taking off a day or two here and there is pretty easy now.
- **Reading for pleasure.** I love to read. If I can't make time to read a physical book, then I can at least listen to the audio version.
- **Listening to podcasts.** If it's about a crime, then I'm spending the time—listening, that is.
- **Playing a game.** Candy Crush, Wordle, and Waffle are my go-to games on my phone when I have a few minutes and need a distraction.
- **Watching a favorite show.** This isn't something I typically do during the day, but if I really need a break or to switch off my brain, a thirty-minute show is a great way to get immersed in something else without spending a ton of time.
- **Puzzles.** I love doing jigsaw puzzles. When I need a break, I head into the dining room and give myself fifteen minutes. It gives me a great opportunity to fully focus on something else and feels like a small win when I find and pop the pieces into place.
- **Going to the dog park.** It's hard to be stressed when you're surrounded by dogs who are thrilled to be there.
- **Coffee with a friend.** This one can be a little tough to squeeze in, but it's worth the effort. Lately, I've been doing Zoom lunch dates with work friends that I can't see in person.
- **Baking.** I don't love baking, but I love eating, so the baking part is sort of required.
- **Doing a chore.** I love doing tasks that don't take long and have concrete endings. Taking a quick break to put laundry in the dryer, load the dishwasher, or even clean a bathroom isn't necessarily a fun way to spend time, but it gets me up and moving and crosses a to-do item off my list, both of which are good.

If there's something that will make you feel better physically on a regular basis, do it. If you have a hobby or favorite activity that will bring you joy and a mental boost, do it. And if you're struggling, reach out and ask for help. If you don't have anyone you can call, then find a group online—or you can even contact me. There are so many resources available, many for free—take advantage of them and take care of yourself.

TAKE THE
Next Step

GOOD

☐ Choose to work in a different location or at a different time today.

☐ Take care of your body by getting annual checkups and getting adequate rest, nutrition, and movement.

BETTER

☐ Find activities that bring you joy and make time each week (or each day!) to do them, even for a short time.

BEST

☐ Schedule time off, let your clients know a few days in advance, set an out-of-office message on your email, and turn off the computer.

Keep up the good work!

Whew! That was a lot. If you're like me, you probably feel overwhelmed or excited or some combination of the two. That's perfectly normal. Whatever you're feeling, wherever you are in your business, take a deep breath. You've got this!

Whether it comes to running my business or doing the actual work I'm paid to do, I often think of the adage, "There is only one way to eat an elephant: one bite at a time." I try to keep that in mind when things feel daunting or there's too much to do or I feel like I don't know what to do next. I start with something small or for a short period, and before I know it I'm well on my way.

My goal is to give you a framework for success and the confidence you need to keep learning as you go. Take it one day at a time, one to-do list item at a time—that's all you need to do.

- Be clear on your goals.
- Connect with good people.
- Work hard.
- Market yourself consistently.
- Stay curious.
- Learn something from every mistake.
- Take care of yourself.
- Find (or create) your network.
- Know where to get help.
- Celebrate often.

Being in business for yourself is incredibly rewarding for so many reasons, especially as a creative, and the best part of being a solopreneur is having the option to pivot and change as you find things that are or aren't working so that you can build the business you want to have. I'd love to hear about your successes and the new lessons you've learned by putting these ideas into practice. If you have any additional questions or challenges, feel free to contact me at goodworkbook.com or LinkedIn (linkedin.com/in/amyweiher).

Good luck!

NOTES

Acknowledgments

This book came to life through generous support of many individuals. I'm grateful to the solopreneurs who shared their authentic stories and insights, enriching these pages with real-world experiences.

To Mike and Cullen: thank you for giving me the time and space to pursue this project. Your understanding as I spent countless hours writing made this book possible. I love you to the moon and back.

To my parents: thank you for keeping me housed and fed when I started working for myself. I wouldn't have had the courage or resources to take the leap without you.

To my beta readers, Teresa Torres and Jill Anderson: your thoughtful feedback shaped this work in essential ways. Gigi Rosenburg and Jill Anderson, my Friday morning "side project" partners, kept me accountable and motivated throughout this journey. And to my mentor Ilise Benun, whose guidance helped me grow both this book and my business: thank you.

My editorial team–Donna Nelson, Melanie Votaw, Amanda Lewis, and Melissa Wuske–provided the expertise needed to refine these words. Linda Secondari and the Studiolo Secondari team transformed the manuscript into the book you hold today.

To the many friends and colleagues who offered encouragement along the way: your support made all the difference.

www.ingramcontent.com/pod-product-compliance
Lightning Source LLC
Chambersburg PA
CBHW040920210326
41597CB00030B/5134